eat!

meat!

peter howard

photography by joe filshie

Lothian
BOOKS

To Gregor Eastham, mate and supporter,

and to the Australian farmers whose produce makes our lives as cooks easier than ever. Through all sorts of circumstances we have the best produce. Sincere thanks to you all.

contents

preface

Growing up in the small Queensland country town of Beaudesert, as I did, there was a constant reminder that all good things come from the earth. The backyard vegetable patch always had something in it that Mum could gather for lunch or dinner, or a relative would drop by with something from the farm. What a way to grow up! Starting life as the consumer of so much great produce, eating well has been a passion of mine ever since I started to cook—which is now many years ago. And one of the exciting things about being in the food industry is that new products are always evolving.

But as we become more and more resource rich and time poor, we find our buying habits are changing too. Often deprived of the luxury of a long yarn with our local butcher, we frequently purchase our meat on the run and tend to stick to a limited range of cuts that we feel confident of cooking well. This is where *Meat!* comes in. This book encourages you to try something different, purchase new cuts of meat, employ unfamiliar cooking techniques. Not only does it provide some new and interesting dishes influenced by Mediterranean, Asian and Middle Eastern flavours, it also mixes in some old favourites of mine. In addition I have included some helpful tips on how to cook those choice meat cuts, no matter what the cooking method, as well as ready-reference charts that tell you the ideal cuts of meat for each cooking technique. So hopefully your next visit to the butcher or the meat section of your supermarket may be better informed.

I remember Margaret Fulton once saying that meats need the respect they so richly deserve. Here in Australia we sometimes take our meat for granted, as we have such ample supplies of everything. But meat does deserve a continuing place in our diets. Besides the fact that the meat industries provide so much employment at home and our primary producers contribute so positively to the country's balance of payments through a healthy export industry and valuable export dollars, meat is still the easiest, most nutritious way to eat for me and mine.

Many people have a role in creating a book such as this, and I would like to take this opportunity to thank them. Publishers become friends—well, so I had heard. Now I discover it is true with Lothian Book's Averill Chase, a dedicated publisher—and friend. Thank you, Averill, for your continued help and trust.

My lovely friend Brenda Oakley went at it again, and as with my last book she proved indispensable for her organisation and administration. Kath Thiess, my next-door neighbour, has done a superb job of testing the recipes to ensure you have a book that is real, approachable and authoritative.

Enjoy!

Peter Howard

8 meat!

introduction

If we tried to compare a typical meal on a family dinner table 50 years ago with one today, we would have some difficulty. It would be easy enough to predict what would be on the table of the past—a hearty meal of meat (probably lamb or beef) with three veg (probably potatoes, carrots and peas)—but the present poses the more difficult assumption. This is because the eating patterns of Australians have changed significantly over the past half century.

So in what ways have our eating patterns changed, and why? The variety of foods we consume has increased enormously over the years, as has our awareness of ingredients, nutrition and safe food practices. Moreover, the cooking techniques we now favour are different to what they were 50 years ago, and the manner in which we eat our food both at home and out of the home has changed. These changes mirror changes to our lifestyle and the higher standard of living we all enjoy today.

The changes to our eating patterns can be attributed to a number of issues. Firstly the make-up of Australian society is radically different now to what it was in the 1950s. While the majority of Australians were of Anglo/Irish/Celtic descent back then, these days the cultural melting pot in which we live is far more diverse. And along with communities from the Mediterranean, the Middle East, South-East Asia and the Pacific, we have welcomed the cuisines of these diverse ethnic groups to our tables. Fifty years ago who would ever have dreamt of whipping up a chicken laksa, beef rendang or even a pizza for dinner. Today we no longer consider meat and three veg the mainstay of our family meal.

Not only have we been influenced by the cuisines of newer Australians, we have also benefited from an increased knowledge and understanding of the health benefits (or otherwise) of certain food groups. As more research has been disseminated about the causes of heart disease, diabetes and high cholesterol, to name but a few, so we have modified our eating habits accordingly.

Leafing through the vast body of food literature that comes regularly across my desk, I am constantly reminded that we are living in the 'lucky country', especially where food is concerned. We are blessed with a bountiful supply of delicious fresh produce, free from many of the health concerns of the old world. This abundance has complemented our changing attitudes to food, as producers have readily responded by developing new and improved meat cuts to suit our health needs, and growers have diversified their crops to meet our desire for more plentiful supplies of once-less-consumed or previously unknown varieties of fruits and vegetables.

Another major influence on our changing eating patterns has been the change in work practices. Mum is no longer expected to stay at home to look after the family's domestic needs, making sure there's a meal waiting for 'the men' on their return home each evening. Now, with most families having two breadwinners and no-one waiting at home with a hot dinner to greet them, an alternative solution for evening meals is being sought. That solution is fast food—pre-prepared, takeaway, or recipes that can turn fresh ingredients into delicious meals in just 15 minutes.

All of these changes have meant challenges for our meat producers. Just as we have said goodbye, by and large, to meat and three veg for dinner each night, so our meat consumption has reduced dramatically. Whether it is because of health concerns, lack of time or simply the adoption of new cuisines that use less meat, we are now faced with generations who have been brought up on a much lower daily intake of meat. With this shift away from meat in our diet and our wholehearted embrace of the one-stop supermarket for all our food supplies, our knowledge and understanding of the many wonderful ways in which meat can be prepared have diminished.

Consequently, folk like Meat & Livestock Australia and other similar groups have been working to increase our awareness of meat and to make sure that not only is our meat safe for us but that it also tastes better. Meat producers have put an enormous amount of work into making sure we can readily identify what cuts are used for what cooking methods. Similar efforts have also been made by our friends at the Pork Corporation and in the poultry industry, all of whom have gone to great lengths to make selecting our meat an easier and more pleasurable experience.

Despite what some may say, meat, whether red or white, is good for us. Without a good portion of meat in our regular diet we may be missing out on some essential nutrients. Meat has always been a rich source of protein, a substance of lifelong importance for growing, repairing and maintaining healthy bodies. Meat also contains valuable nutrients such as thiamine (B1), riboflavin (B2) and nicotinic acid (niacin), which help the body produce energy from the food it consumes. While lamb, beef and pork all have similar nutritional value, pork is richer in thiamine, and lamb and beef are excellent sources of bio-available iron, vitamin B12 and zinc. Chicken, duck, turkey and quail are also high in protein but much lower in saturated fats. Chicken is a very good source of unsaturated fatty acids that are useful in the fight against cholesterol.

In Australia, a lot of the meat we eat is 'grass-fed', which means the animal has to roam to eat. This ensures that the muscles are used, with the result that the animals do not store as much fat as stationary ones such as those in feed lots. Recent research also tells us that lean beef, lamb and veal provide us with valuable levels of omega-3 fats, known to play an important part in the health of our heart, blood vessels and brain. This gives Australians a health advantage straightaway. If red meat is trimmed of all visible selvedge fat, it can be very lean. My butcher will trim all the visible fat from the cuts I buy while I stand there having a chat and contemplating the rest of the order.

For me, as someone who has been involved in the food industry for over 35 years, the nutritional aspects of eating meat are important. But just as important is the fact that the meats we eat are flavoursome. They must also be affordable and versatile. And they must be cooked to their best advantage. We often blame the product when it is we who have affected the flavour of the dish because of the way we have cooked it, either because of previous experiences or tradition. Too often we overcook our meats, which leaves them dry and uninteresting. Boneless chicken breast, for example, requires careful cooking to keep it moist and tender, not overcooked and dry.

Special occasions require special dinners, and what better way to celebrate than with a properly cooked piece of meat? Meat has always signified the generosity of the table and what it offers.

Meat of all descriptions is a part of the Australian way of life and we can still be assured of being able to purchase a diverse range of cuts to suit our purposes. We consumers get it extremely easy in this country of ours, which provides us with a bountiful table and a lifestyle unmatched anywhere else in the world. So make the most of it. Put a little meat back on your plate.

starters
and salads

get the gastro juices flowing

In my days as a restaurateur, writing the starter course of the menu somehow always seemed the easiest. And for my guests, choosing a starter was easy too. (It was only come the main course that decision dilemmas set in!)

All this stands to reason, because the food and wine served at the beginning of a meal is designed to get the gastro juices flowing and set you up for a great time. Starters are seen as being interesting and inviting—after all, we are all ravenous at this time.

Dishes at the start of a meal need to be cleansing, inviting, versatile and, more and more, substantial, as they can sometimes be all folk want. Meeting these diverse requirements has been made easier and more interesting with the use of the myriad of Asian flavours that titillate and tantalise the palate.

Meat is an important component of each dish for this part of the meal. Here you will find canapés, appetisers and entrées—some casual, some dressed up and some ready-to-go as dinners.

oregano *lamb and beef balls*

1 Combine all the ingredients except for the vegetable oil and mix well using your hands. Season with salt and pepper. With wet hands, roll the mixture into balls approximately 2.5 cm in diameter. Store on a plate lined with plastic wrap and, when done, cover and refrigerate for 1 hour before use.

2 Heat the oil in a large frying pan and shallow-fry the balls, turning regularly, until done. Lift out and drain on kitchen towels. Serve when cool enough to handle.

MAKES APPROXIMATELY 50

500 g equal parts lamb and beef mince

1 medium-sized onion, finely chopped

1 medium-sized green chilli, seeded and chopped

$1/2$ cup chopped fresh oregano

$1/2$ teaspoon garam masala

$1/4$ teaspoon dried oregano

1 teaspoon white sugar

$1/2$ cup dried breadcrumbs

1 egg, beaten

vegetable oil, for cooking

cool *chilli chicken* on mushroom pancakes

for the chicken

2 medium-sized chicken breast fillets

100 g chicken mince

1 small red chilli, seeded and
   roughly chopped

10 fresh coriander leaves

for the pancakes

1 egg

$1/2$ cup (125 ml) milk

$3/4$ cup self-raising flour, sifted

$1/2$ teaspoon ground coriander

vegetable oil, for cooking

4–6 button mushrooms, stalks
   removed and finely sliced

sweet chilli sauce

coriander leaves (optional)

Around my place, we do lots of home entertaining and I always like to have something to nibble on prior to the meal. This recipe became a favourite because it was so versatile: not only is it a great starter, it also converts to picnics and mains very easily.

PREHEAT OVEN TO 180°C

1 Prepare the chicken breasts by butterflying each one to make as flat as possible. Mix the chicken mince and chilli together, tear up the coriander leaves as finely as possible and combine with the mince mixture.

2 Spoon the mixture down the centre of each chicken breast, then roll the meat around the filling to make the filling as centred as possible. Tie with string or use toothpicks to skewer into place. Steam or bake in the oven, covered with foil, for 20–30 minutes. When done, leave to cool, then refrigerate until ready to use.

3 Make the pancakes by mixing the egg and milk, then stir in the flour and ground coriander and work to a batter. Heat a little oil in a frying pan and make pancakes to a size to suit round slices of chicken. When bubbles start to appear, press a few slices of mushroom on top of each pancake. Flip the pancakes over and continue cooking until lightly browned. Cook until all the batter is used.

4 Slice the chicken into thin rounds. Spread a little sweet chilli sauce over the top of the pancakes (this stops chicken slices slipping off) and top with a slice or two of the chicken. Decorate with chopped coriander leaves if you like.

parmesan-crusted *chicken tenderloins*

SERVES 4

500 g chicken tenderloins

2 cups fresh breadcrumbs

$1/2$ cup finely grated Parmesan
cheese

1 cup plain flour mixed with
$1/2$ teaspoon salt and $1/2$ teaspoon
black pepper

1 egg, beaten

vegetable oil, for shallow-frying

1 Trim the chicken tenderloins of fat or gristle and refrigerate until ready for use. Mix the breadcrumbs and cheese together and put into a deep plate.

2 Prepare the chicken by placing the flour, salt and pepper mix in a plastic bag and then dropping in a few tenderloins at a time. Shake, lift the chicken out and shake off the excess flour.

3 Dip the tenderloins into the egg. Lift out and coat with the breadcrumbs. This is best done by shaking the plate so the crumbs come up around the side of the chicken. Flip the chicken over and then pat the crumbs onto the pieces. Lift out with a fork and rest on a plate.

4 Heat the oil in a large frying pan and, when a few crumbs dance in the oil when dropped in, add the chicken tenderloins, in batches. Cook until lightly browned, turning only once. Lift out and place onto kitchen towels. Always let the oil reheat before you add another batch of chicken.

5 Serve hot with a green salad or cold as a canapé.

TIP

Shallow-frying is easy to do and the food tells you when it is ready to be turned over or taken out. When you first put the item in a small amount of oil to be cooked, the bubbles around the outside are large. When the bubbles become smaller, this is an indication that the item is ready to be turned or lifted out.

deep-fried garlic and *chilli beef*

1 Trim the rump steak of all fat and cut into fine, long strips. Set to one side.

2 Mix the soy sauce, sugar, rice wine and allspice. Stir to dissolve the sugar and whisk in enough cornflour to form a thin paste about the consistency of runny cream. Tip the steak strips into the mixture and leave to sit for 1 hour.

3 Pour at least 6 cm of oil into a suitable saucepan and heat to very hot. Lift out some of the strips and carefully put them into the oil. They will cook very quickly. When floating, lift out and drain. Keep them warm and repeat the process until all the beef is done.

4 In a wok over high heat, dry-cook the garlic and chillies for 30 seconds, or until the garlic has started to brown. Add the cooked beef and Sichuan pepper, toss quickly to combine and tip out onto a serving plate. Serve with soy sauce for dipping.

SERVES 4

400 g rump steak, 2 cm thick

3 tablespoons soy sauce

1 tablespoon brown sugar

2 tablespoons rice wine

1 tablespoon Chinese allspice

1–2 tablespoons cornflour

peanut or vegetable oil, for frying

3 cloves garlic, sliced

3 small red chillies, seeded and chopped

Sichuan pepper, to taste

soy sauce, for dipping

ham, cumin and couscous cakes

MAKES 16–18

$^3/_4$ cup dried couscous

$^1/_2$ cup finely diced ham

1 tablespoon minced green onions

2 cloves garlic, minced

1 egg, beaten

1 tablespoon plain flour

1 teaspoon baharat

1 teaspoon salt

1 tablespoon chopped fresh chives

vegetable oil, for pan-frying

sour cream mixed with grated
  cucumber flesh (optional)

spinach, rocket and cashew nut
  pesto (optional—see Basics
  page 136)

Spices have fascinated me ever since my childhood—seeing the different spices that went into the Christmas cakes and puddings had me intrigued. It still does. Baharat is a spice mixture from the Middle East. It is a blend made with paprika, pepper, cumin, cassia, cloves, coriander, cardamom and nutmeg.

1 Mix the couscous with 1 cup (250 ml) of boiling water. Combine with all the other ingredients, except the oil, sour cream/cucumber and pesto, and mix well.

2 Heat the oil in a pan for frying. With wet hands, roll one heaped tablespoon of the mixture into a ball, then flatten the ball into a patty shape and cook on both sides until browned—about 1–2 minutes each side. Lift out of the pan and onto kitchen towels and continue making and cooking the cakes until all the mixture is used up.

3 Serve on their own, topped with sour cream mixed with grated cucumber flesh, or with spinach, rocket and cashew nut pesto.

kromeskies

150 g mixed cooked meats (say pork,
  lamb, veal or chicken)

30 g butter

2 tablespoons diced bacon

1 small onion, finely chopped

2 tablespoons plain flour

150 ml milk, warmed

1 tablespoon chopped fresh
  curly-leaf parsley

$1/2$ teaspoon finely grated nutmeg

for the batter

1 cup plain flour, sifted

1 tablespoon olive oil

1 egg white, lightly beaten

vegetable oil, for shallow-frying

lemon, for squeezing

spinach, rocket and cashew nut
  pesto (see Basics page 136)

I always remember these—they were one of the delicious
things I cooked at East Sydney Food School in 1970. My
Hungarian chef teacher, Alex Chovan, loved them, and so
did I. They are a great way to use leftover meats and vegies,
and they are so simple to make.

1 Dice the meats finely and mix well.

2 Melt the butter in a saucepan over medium heat and cook the bacon
   and onion for 2 minutes. Stir in the flour and cook for 1 minute—
   the flour should be going a blond colour as you stir. Tip the milk
   in gradually and stir to combine. Add the mixed meats, parsley and
   nutmeg and cook over low heat until the mixture thickens. Remove,
   cool and refrigerate.

3 For the batter, put the flour in a bowl, then whisk in the oil and
   150 ml of warm water until small bubbles appear. Add the egg
   white just before use and fold in.

4 Heat the oil in a frying pan. When a small drop of the batter dances
   across the top of it, you are ready to cook. Scoop a dessertspoonful of
   the meat mixture and shape into a longish sausage. Dip in the batter
   and fry until golden in colour; lift from the oil and drain on kitchen
   towels. Continue making and cooking kromeskies until all the mixture
   is used up.

5 Serve with a squeeze of lemon and a bowl of spinach, rocket and
   cashew nut pesto.

chicken, *black-eye beans and lettuce soup*

1 Trim all excess fat from the chicken thigh fillets and cut into thick strips.

2 Heat the oil in a large frying pan and add the onion, celery and chicken strips. Stir for 2 minutes and add the beans, chicken stock, Worcestershire sauce and anchovy sauce. Bring to a simmer and cook for 45–60 minutes, or until the beans are softened.

3 When nearly ready, add salt and pepper to taste and cook a further 5 minutes.

4 Shred the lettuce very finely and place even amounts in the bottom of large soup bowls. When ready to serve, ensure the soup is very hot and ladle it over the lettuce. Decorate with marjoram and serve with herbed bread.

SERVES 4

4 large chicken thigh fillets

1 tablespoon vegetable oil

1 large onion, roughly chopped

1 stick celery, string removed and roughly chopped

1 cup dried black-eye beans, soaked overnight in water

4 cups (1 L) chicken stock (see Basics page 130)

2 tablespoons Worcestershire sauce

1 tablespoon anchovy sauce

$1/2$ small iceberg lettuce, washed

4 large sprigs fresh marjoram

pork balls *in a star anise broth*

for the pork balls

200 g lean pork mince, finely minced

1 tablespoon minced green onions

$1/4$ teaspoon ground coriander

$1/2$ teaspoon fish sauce

1 tablespoon plain flour

2 tablespoons finely chopped water
  chestnuts

for the broth

4 star anise, cracked open

1 teaspoon Sichuan peppercorns,
  cracked

1 teaspoon dried fennel seeds

1 tablespoon roughly chopped fresh
  ginger

1 small dried red chilli, broken open

8 cups (2 L) chicken stock
  (see Basics page 130)

$1/4$ cup (60 ml) rice wine or dry sherry

2 small pieces dried mandarin skin

100–200 g cooked rice vermicelli

sesame oil

The inspiration for this stunning soup comes from the masterly hands of Christine Manfield, who has cooked great food for years. Paramount Restaurant, run by her and her partner Margie, was a mecca for superb dining.

1 Make the pork balls by mixing all the pork balls ingredients together. With wet hands, roll into small balls and put onto a plate. Cover with plastic wrap and refrigerate for at least 1 hour.

2 Make the broth by combining all the broth ingredients in a large saucepan. Bring to the boil, reduce the heat and simmer for 45 minutes.

3 Strain the broth into another saucepan. In the original saucepan, bring enough water to the boil to blanch the pork balls. In small batches, plunge the balls into the water and cook for 1 minute. Lift out.

4 Reheat the broth, add the blanched balls and cook for 20 minutes on slow heat. The balls must be cooked through. Serve ladled over freshly cooked rice vermicelli, with 2 drops of sesame oil dripped in each bowl as you serve.

smoked *pork hock* and sweet potato soup

SERVES 4–6

1 large smoked pork hock, split
  lengthwise

1 tablespoon light olive oil

1 medium-sized onion, roughly
  chopped

2 sticks celery, washed, trimmed
  and roughly chopped

1 medium-sized carrot,
  peeled and roughly chopped

500 g kumera (orange sweet potato),
  peeled and roughly chopped

chicken stock (see Basics page 130)

$1/4$ teaspoon cayenne pepper

200 g sour cream

1 Place the pork hock in a large saucepan, cover with water and bring
  to the boil. Reduce the heat and simmer for 1 hour. Remove from the
  heat, lift the pork out with a slotted spoon and leave to cool. Remove
  the skin from the meat and chop the meat roughly. Set to one side.

2 In another saucepan, heat the oil and quickly fry the onion, celery
  and carrot for 2 minutes. Add the sweet potato and pour over enough
  chicken stock to cover. Bring to a simmer and cook for 45 minutes,
  or until the vegetables are breaking up.

3 Remove from the heat and add the cayenne pepper. With a hand-held
  blender, purée the vegetables in the saucepan.

4 Add the pork meat and return the soup to low heat. Cook slowly for
  15 minutes, stirring regularly. Check the seasoning and add salt
  and more cayenne if required. Serve in individual bowls with a good
  spoonful of sour cream.

warm *thai beef* salad

There are so many variations on this superb Thai salad—and this is one more that I have adapted to available ingredients.

PREHEAT GRILL OR BARBECUE TO VERY HOT

1 Combine the chilli, sugar, lime zest and juice and fish sauce. Pound or mix well, either using a mortar and pestle or the back of a dessertspoon to release the aroma of the lime. When mixed, tip into a large bowl.

2 Trim the meat of all fat. Spray or brush the grill or barbecue with a little oil and seal the steak for 1 minute each side. Ideally the beef should be rare, but if you prefer, cook it further.

3 When cooked, remove the beef and let it sit for 5 minutes, then cut across the grain into fine slices. Retain the juices. Lift the shredded meat into the lime mixture and toss gently. Leave to sit for a minute and then toss with the green onions, basil, mint and coriander leaves.

4 Arrange the mixed lettuce leaves on plates and evenly distribute the beef on top of the leaves. Sprinkle with the peanuts and serve immediately.

SERVES 4

1 small red chilli, seeded and finely sliced

1 teaspoon brown sugar

grated zest an juice of 1 lime

2 tablespoons fish sauce

500 g lean beef (fillet, rump, sirloin or similar steak), cut in 2 cm thick slices

vegetable oil spray

2 green onions, trimmed and sliced finely on the diagonal

1 cup fresh Thai basil or regular basil leaves

$1/2$ cup fresh mint or spearmint leaves

$1/2$ cup fresh coriander leaves

mixed lettuce leaves (preferably an Asian mix if available), washed

2 tablespoons chopped dry-roasted unsalted peanuts

chicken and ham *choi bao*

SERVES 4

150 g ham, minced or finely diced

400 g chicken mince

1 tablespoon vegetable oil

3 cloves garlic, finely chopped

$1/2$ cup (125 ml) hoisin sauce

100 g water chestnuts, drained and
  roughly chopped

1 tablespoon fresh coriander leaves,
  finely torn or chopped

for the sauce

2 tablespoons sweet chilli sauce

2 tablespoons light soy sauce

1 tablespoon lime juice

8 medium-sized lettuce leaves,
  washed and crisped

This deliciously spicy ham and chicken dish served in crisp lettuce cups is one of the old-time favourites of Asian food. It is very simple to prepare, and once you start eating it you really won't want to stop. This recipe makes four very large servings.

1 Mix the ham and chicken together and keep to one side.

2 In a wok over high heat, bring the oil to smoking point and add the garlic. Stir for 5 seconds and add the mixed meats. Using the back of a large spoon or a wok spatula, mash the meat so it does not go lumpy. Pour in the hoisin sauce and $1/2$ cup (125 ml) of water, then add the water chestnuts. Cook for 5 minutes, stirring constantly. Add the coriander and stir in.

3 To make the sauce, mix together the sweet chilli sauce, soy sauce and lime juice.

4 Serve the choi bao in a large bowl in the middle of the table with the lettuce cups and sauce to one side.

TIP

It is sometimes difficult to get enough lettuce-leaf cups from a regular lettuce and so I can highly recommend that you use cos lettuce. The individual leaves are removed from the stem, trimmed, washed and crisped in the refrigerator. They are shaped more like boats than cups, but they are much easier to handle.

potted beef, *beetroot terrine and salad*

This dish comes in and out of fashion. Right now, anything to do with jellies is in.
This modern adaptation of a classic recipe is flavour-packed and texturally stunning.

1   Place the beef, pork, star anise and mandarin skin in a large pot and cover with water. Bring to the boil. Reduce the heat and skim off the froth as it forms. Simmer for 4 hours, or cook in a very slow oven for 5–6 hours.

2   Remove from the heat and cool. Lift out the meat; strain the broth, cool and refrigerate overnight. When the meat is cooled, trim all the fat and gristle off it and chop very finely. Cover and refrigerate overnight.

3   Lift all fat off the top of the now jellied broth and bring the broth back to the boil. Boil, uncovered, for 30 minutes, then return the meat to the boiling broth.

4   Cook for 15 minutes and then add the anchovy essence, pepper, mustard and vinegar. Bring back to the boil and cook for a further 5 minutes.

5   Lift off the heat and rip the cooked meat to fine shreds using the tines of two forks. Spoon out into a large glass bowl, or into a terrine or loaf tin, that has been rinsed out with cold water. Refrigerate until set, then turn out onto a board and cut into 2 cm thick slices.

6 Assemble the salad by starting with the lettuce leaves as a base on individual plates. Tumble equal amounts of potato and artichoke hearts onto the lettuce. Place a slice of beetroot terrine to one side and top the lettuce base with slices of the potted beef. Sprinkle with the diced cucumber.

7 Mix the mayonnaise with the plum sauce and add enough water to thin to a drizzling consistency. Spoon over the meat and other ingredients and sprinkle with lemon pepper.

TIP

To serve potted beef as a canapé, spoon suitable amounts into pastry or bread cases and sprinkle with a little diced cucumber.

SERVES 4

for the potted beef

2.5 kg shin beef on the bone, thickly sliced

1 kg salted belly pork

2 star anise

1 piece dried mandarin skin

2 tablespoons anchovy essence

1 teaspoon ground white pepper

2 tablespoons English mustard

2 tablespoons balsamic vinegar

mixed lettuce leaves, washed and crisped

4 small potatoes, sliced into 1 cm thick pieces and boiled until tender (run under cold water to stop cooking)

4 artichoke hearts, halved

4 x 2 cm thick slices jellied beetroot and coriander terrine (see Basics page 139)

1 finely diced cucumber, peeled and seeded

$1/2$ cup mayonnaise

2 tablespoons Asian plum sauce

cracked lemon pepper

smoked turkey, *bocconcini and pumpkin shards*

200 g smoked turkey, finely sliced

8 small bocconcini

400 g pumpkin (preferably butternut)

1 tablespoon olive oil

$1/2$ teaspoon freshly grated nutmeg

$1/2$ teaspoon powdered chilli

1 tablespoon balsamic vinegar

2 tablespoons extra-virgin olive oil

mixed salad leaves, washed and
  crisped

8 halves semi-roasted tomatoes,
  cut into halves

PREHEAT OVEN TO 200°C

1 Separate the turkey slices into four even amounts. Cut the bocconcini into halves.

2 Using the top of the butternut pumpkin (the firm part with no seeds), cut round slices 1–2 cm thick and then cut into shards or wedges.

3 Heat the oil in a roasting pan, add the pumpkin and sprinkle with the nutmeg, powdered chilli and salt and pepper to taste. Toss the pumpkin so as to coat with the spices and oil. Cook in the oven for 25–30 minutes, turning a couple of times to brown all over.

4 Remove the pumpkin from the oven, cool for 1 minute and pour over the vinegar and extra-virgin olive oil. Toss and leave to sit for 30 minutes.

5 Assemble the salad by putting a base of mixed salad leaves in the centre of each plate. Add the bocconcini, plus some of the pumpkin, tomatoes and turkey, and repeat until all the ingredients are used. Spoon any of the remaining vinegar and oil mixture over the salads to taste.

deep-fried quails *with deep-fried silverbeet and sesame seeds*

SERVES 4

4 quails

1 tablespoon Chinese allspice

1 teaspoon salt

$1/2$ teaspoon ground white pepper

peanut oil, for deep-frying

8 silverbeet leaves, white rib
  removed, washed and well dried

1 teaspoon sea salt

1 tablespoon white sugar

1 tablespoon sesame seeds

Asian plum sauce

1 Cut the quails into quarters by firstly cutting the birds down the backbone and then cutting through the breastbones. Slice the hindquarters from the breasts. Wash and drain on kitchen towels.

2 Mix the allspice, salt and pepper well. Heat 6 cm of oil in a wok and, when hot enough to deep-fry, sprinkle the quail cuts liberally with the allspice mixture and drop into the oil. Cook in batches until browned and cooked through—about 2–3 minutes. When done, keep in a warm place.

3 Shred the silverbeet leaves as finely as you can. Plunge batches of the silverbeet into the oil and, when floating, scoop out onto kitchen towels (it cooks really quickly, so be ready to lift it out with a slotted spoon almost immediately). When all done, tip into a bowl and sprinkle with salt and sugar. Toss well and then sprinkle with sesame seeds.

4 Serve the silverbeet on a suitable round plate with the quails on another, and serve the plum sauce separately.

prosciutto, semi-roasted tomatoes and feta salad

PREHEAT GRILL TO HOT

1 Grill the prosciutto until crisp—do this on aluminium foil punched with holes to let the liquid drain out. If the prosciutto is left to sit in its own juices, it will not crisp. Lift and drain on kitchen towels. Allow to cool.

2 Assemble the salad by placing the salad leaves in a large salad bowl. Tumble in the tomatoes, potatoes, green onions, pepitas and feta cheese.

3 Make the dressing by whisking the oil and slowly drizzling in the sherry vinegar. Season with salt and pepper to taste.

4 Pour the dressing over the salad and toss. Sprinkle with the chopped parsley, put the crisp prosciutto on top and serve immediately. You may like to crumble the prosciutto, but I prefer it left in whole slices.

SERVES 4

8 slices prosciutto

mixed salad leaves, washed and ripped into bite-sized pieces

12–16 semi-roasted tomatoes, in quarters

4 medium-sized cooked potatoes, skins on and cut into bite-sized pieces

2 green onions, trimmed and cut into 3 cm lengths

$1/4$ cup pepitas, lightly roasted

100 g feta cheese, roughly diced

$1/4$ cup (60 ml) extra-virgin olive oil

2 tablespoons sherry vinegar

2 tablespoons chopped fresh curly-leaf parsley

bacon, *peach and blue cheese salad*

4 medium-sized bacon rashers,
  rinds removed

2 peaches, washed and each one
  cut into eight wedges

juice of 1 small lemon

mixed salad leaves, washed

1 red capsicum, roasted, seeds
  removed and cut into strips

2 green onions, trimmed and cut
  into 3 cm lengths

$1/2$ cup blue-vein cheese

$1/4$ cup (60 ml) orange juice

2 tablespoons chopped fresh chives

PREHEAT GRILL TO HOT

1 Grill or barbecue the bacon until crisp and the fat is removed;
   drain on kitchen towels and cool.

2 Put the peach slices into a bowl and mix with the lemon juice to
   stop browning. (If using immediately, leave out the lemon juice.)

3 Assemble the salad by placing the salad leaves in a large bowl and
   tumbling with the capsicum and green onion pieces. Drain the peach
   wedges and add to the salad. The bacon can either be crumbled into
   the salad or left in large pieces. If you choose the latter method, leave
   the bacon to one side and place on top of the salad once it is dressed
   and tossed. If crumbling, do so now.

4 Make the dressing by mashing the cheese with the orange juice and
   ground black pepper to taste. It will be a slightly lumpy dressing.
   Pour over the salad and toss, sprinkle with the chopped chives and
   serve with good bread.

stir-fries
and sautés

how easy are they!

I often wonder where we were before the stir-fry came into everyday use. Stir-fries are so often lifesavers—how easy are they!

As a TV cook, I would be lost without these quick dishes. After all, a good stir-fry can come together within the minutes allocated to me for live TV cooking. Also, the flamboyance that a stir-fry allows in demonstration cooking never ceases to hold the audience's imagination.

The term 'sauté' is the European equivalent to the Asian stir-fry, as it means to cook quickly while moving the ingredients around the pan, generally referred to as a 'sauteuse'. This method of cooking was one of my favourites in the restaurant kitchens in which I cooked. Its quickness made the dishes easy to prepare and present. Consequently, the customers always felt that the sautéed dish had been specially cooked there and then for them—and it had been.

It is said that nearly every house in Australia has a wok. I have collected many of them over the years. I have one from chef Yan (an amazing man with whom I worked in Hong Kong), chef Ken Hom (who appeared twice with me during my 'Midday Show' days), and I am hanging out to get one from that fantastic Australian, Elizabeth Chong, who I have worked with so many times.

I, like so many Aussies, have adapted to the quick method of cooking that is stir-frying and sautéing.

tips for stir-fries and sautés

- Have all ingredients ready for use—there is not time for you to be cutting or peeling once the wok is hot. This is fast cooking and needs your full attention.
- Have the ingredients cut small and of equal size so they cook quickly and evenly.
- Layer the foodstuffs in the wok. Those ingredients that take longer to cook, say onion, celery, carrots and meat, need to be the first in, while the greens nearly always go in last.
- Pans and woks need to be very hot and as such need to be made from thinner metals so they will conduct the heat more quickly. Heavy-based pans retain heat too long for something that needs instant heat and needs to lose it as quickly as it is gained.
- The oil used in a wok will form a haze as it heats. Don't worry, you're not burning the oil. Elizabeth Chong refers to this haze as 'the breath of the wok' and it signifies that the cooking can start.
- When adding liquid to a wok, always pour it down the sides, not right into the middle—doing this takes all the heat from the wok and stops the cooking momentarily.

IDEAL CUTS FOR STIR-FRIES AND SAUTÉS

Meats listed here should be prepared as outlined in the recipes. This enables them to be cooked quickly, which is the essence of stir-frying and sautéing.

LAMB	BEEF	VEAL	POULTRY	PORK
Boneless loin	Rump steak	Schnitzel steak	Duck breast (boneless)	Fillet
Chump chops	Scotch fillet	Cutlets	Turkey breast	Boneless loin
Leg chops	Sirloin	Tenderloin	Chicken breast fillet	Spare ribs (belly)
Tenderloin (fillets)	Oyster blade		Chicken thigh fillet	Sausages
Cutlets	Eye round		Chicken thigh cutlet	
	Sausages			
	Tenderloin			

soy lamb, *mushroom and broccolini stir-fry*

2 tablespoons soy sauce

2 tablespoons honey

1 tablespoon oyster sauce

1 small red chilli, seeded and finely chopped

400 g boneless lamb fillet or loin, finely sliced

2 tablespoons peanut oil

1 small onion, cut into wedges

250 g button mushrooms, roughly chopped

1 small bunch broccolini, washed and chopped

1 small red capsicum, seeded and finely sliced

New ingredients come to us all the time, and being able to adapt them to familiar dishes is the essence of an innovative cuisine. Broccolini is a hybrid cross of broccoli and choy sum. Mushrooms are old friends, and lamb used in a stir-fry is very Australian.

1 Mix the soy sauce, honey and oyster sauce with the chilli. Add the lamb and toss to coat. Lift the lamb from the marinade and reserve the liquid.

2 In a wok, heat half the oil to smoking point and quickly seal the lamb slices (this will need to be done in two batches). Keep the lamb warm and pour in the remaining oil. Bring up to smoking point.

3 Add the onion and mushrooms, cook for 1 minute and then tip in the broccolini and capsicum. Cook for a further 2 minutes before returning the lamb to the wok, along with the reserved lamb marinade. Cook until the capsicum is wilted but still crunchy. Sometimes you may need to add just a splash of water to help with the cooking process. Add only a small amount.

4 Serve immediately with steamed or boiled rice.

stir-fry lamb *and eggplant*

2 tablespoons vegetable oil

500 g boneless loin of lamb, cut into
   thin strips

250 g eggplant, in 2 cm dice

1 x 5 cm piece lemongrass, white
   part only

1 small red chilli, seeded and
   chopped

juice of 1 lime

2 teaspoons white sugar

2 tablespoons tamarind paste

1 x 3 cm piece fresh ginger, peeled
   and minced

1 tablespoon fish sauce

1 tablespoon soy sauce

2 medium-sized green onions, cut
   into 3 cm pieces on the diagonal

1 In a wok, heat the oil to smoking point and seal the lamb in batches.
   When lightly brown, lift out with a slotted spoon, leaving as much oil
   in the wok as possible.

2 Add more oil to the wok if necessary and cook the eggplant until
   lightly browned. Lift out with a slotted spoon and bring the oil in the
   wok back to smoking point. You may need to add a little more oil.

3 Tip in the lemongrass, chilli, lime juice, sugar, tamarind paste,
   ginger, fish and soy sauces and the green onion. Cook while
   stirring for 1 minute. You may need to add a little water to help
   with the cooking.

4 Return the lamb and eggplant to the wok and toss and stir for
   5 minutes or until everything is cooked to your liking.

5 Serve over cooked noodles of your choice.

my special *savoury mince*

We used to be served savoury mince at boarding college—nothing like my mother's, nor this one, which I have come to love. It can be eaten as is with vegetables and is stunning topped with mashed potatoes, dotted with butter and baked until golden brown. But for now, the basic recipe…

1 Bring the oil to medium heat in a frying pan and add the butter. When foaming, add the onion and cook for 1 minute, then add the mince and mash to ensure it does not go lumpy.

2 Sprinkle with the flour and stir in. Add the milk and stir to combine.

3 Add the herbs and sugar and simmer for 30 minutes. When the savoury mince is ready, season with salt and white pepper and serve with lashings of steamed potatoes and vegetables, with the chopped oregano sprinkled over the top.

SERVES 4–6

2 tablespoons vegetable oil

1 tablespoon butter

1 medium-sized onion, finely chopped

600 g lean beef mince

2 tablespoons plain flour

1 cup (250 ml) milk

1 tablespoon dried mixed herbs

1 tablespoon white sugar

1 teaspoon salt

$1/2$ teaspoon ground white pepper

2 tablespoons chopped fresh oregano

sautéed chinese *pepper-crusted lamb* with bok choy

SERVES 4

4 x 150 g boneless loins of lamb

1 tablespoon Sichuan peppercorns

$1/2$ teaspoon salt

2 tablespoons vegetable oil

8 baby bok choy, washed and
   quartered with the leaves removed
   and retained

2 tablespoons oyster sauce

1 tablespoon soy sauce

$1/2$ teaspoon flaked dried red chilli

2 tablespoons lamb stock (see
   Basics page 131) or water

100 g snow pea sprouts

The peppercorns used here are the Chinese Sichuan ones. They have a little sweetness in them that I find very appealing. This simple dish lets the lamb do its own thing, the pepper adding that little bite.

1 Trim the lamb if necessary—it is crucial that all the 'silver' be removed in order to prevent the meat from distorting during cooking. Crush the Sichuan peppercorns in a mortar and pestle with the salt, then sprinkle it over the lamb loins. Pat it into the lamb and leave to sit while the oil heats.

2 In a large pan, heat the oil until very hot, then add the lamb. Do not prod or disturb the meat for 1 minute, then turn and cook undisturbed for another minute. Turn the heat down to medium and cook the meat until done. I prefer this cut of meat cooked to medium, which will take about 3–4 minutes each side. Lift out and allow to sit for 5 minutes.

3 Reheat the same pan and add the whites of the bok choy only. Tip in the oyster and soy sauces and add the chilli flakes and a little stock or water to help with the cooking. When the stems are near done (they should still have some crunch), add the sprouts and the bok choy leaves and toss around in the pan. Remove from the heat almost immediately, as the greens will still cook as you slice the meat.

4 Slice the meat on the diagonal and across the grain so as to get some longish strips. Spoon the greens onto the centre of the plates and top with slices of the lamb. Spoon over the sauce from the bok choy and serve with cooked noodles of your choice.

sauté of chicken with lemon myrtle and dried fig sauce

SERVES 4

4 x 150 g chicken breast fillets

2 tablespoons vegetable oil

2 green onions, trimmed and finely chopped

$1/2$ cup (125 ml) dry white wine

$1/2$ cup (125 ml) cream

1 tablespoon preserved Japanese pickled (pink) ginger

2 dried figs, finely diced

$1/2$ teaspoon powdered lemon myrtle

cayenne pepper, to taste

Every now and then I get an urge to tart up something really easy to make a dress-up dish. Chicken breast meat is my versatile base for this delicious sauté. Lemon myrtle—the special ingredient of the dish—is now available in good supermarkets and delis. Failing that, you can always get it by mail order from my old mate Ian Hemphill. The web site is www.herbies.com.

1 Cut the chicken breasts into halves lengthways (through their thinnest part) and pat flat with a meat mallet. The best way to do this is to place the slices between plastic wrap and hit gently. They do not need to be thin, just flat enough to allow even cooking.

2 In a large frying pan, heat the oil to medium and pan-fry the chicken pieces until lightly browned. Lift out onto a warm plate and keep warm.

3 Bring the heat up high and sauté the green onions for 1 minute. Carefully pour in the wine and cream and bring to the boil.

4 Add the ginger, diced fig and lemon myrtle and simmer for 3–5 minutes. Sprinkle in salt and cayenne pepper to taste and return the chicken to the pan, along with the reserved juices from the plate. Move the chicken around the pan, coating it with the sauce.

5 Serve with cooked pasta and grilled zucchini halves.

tamarind *chicken* curry

1 Soak the tamarind pulp in $1/2$ (125ml) of warm water and allow
  to cool before straining to reserve the liquid. Mix the reserved liquid
  with the curry paste and pour over the chicken meat. Leave to soak
  for 2 hours.

2 Heat the oil and fry the curry leaves, onion, garlic and ginger until
  light brown in colour. Tip in the chicken and tamarind juice and
  simmer for 20 minutes.

3 Pour in the coconut milk and cook for a further 5 minutes. Check
  for seasoning—you may need to add some salt.

4 Serve with boiled long-grain rice.

SERVES 4

2 tablespoons tamarind paste

2 tablespoons peanut green curry
  paste (see Basics page 138)

600 g chicken thigh fillets,
  roughly cubed

3 tablespoons vegetable oil

4 fresh curry leaves (or 2 if dried)

1 large onion, finely chopped

4 cloves garlic, crushed

1 tablespoon minced fresh ginger

1 cup (250 ml) coconut milk

chicken and scallop sauté with vermicelli noodles

SERVES 4

2 cups (500 ml) peanut oil

plain flour, for dusting

300 g chicken breast fillets, cut
   cross-wise into even, roundish
   slices

16 large scallops (roe on), vein
   removed from the side of the
   scallops

200 ml coconut cream

2 cloves garlic, crushed

$1/2$ teaspoon minced fresh ginger

2 kaffir lime leaves, vein removed
   and finely shredded

5 sprigs fresh coriander, finely torn
   or chopped

2 teaspoons fish sauce

$1/2$ teaspoon sesame oil

2 teaspoons white sugar

juice of 1 small lemon

cooked rice vermicelli noodles

fresh coriander leaves, for
   garnishing

This fragrant dish combines ingredients from the land and the sea beautifully. It is served with versatile vermicelli noodles, also known as rice-stick noodles. Noodles play a major part in our eating life these days, and a book I often refer to is Terry Durack's *Noodle*, which gives a complete breakdown on these indispensable Asian ingredients.

1 Heat the oil in a large wok. Place the flour in a plastic bag, drop the chicken into it and shake to dust the chicken. Lift out gently, shake excess flour from the chicken and put the meat into the wok. Stir to cook quickly but do not brown.

2 Lift the chicken out and quickly seal the scallops in the same oil; lift them out to sit on some kitchen towels. Discard the oil and return the wok to medium heat. Add the coconut cream, garlic, ginger, kaffir lime leaves, coriander, fish sauce, sesame oil, sugar and lemon juice. Bring to a simmer and return the chicken to the wok. Simmer for 10 minutes or until the chicken is cooked. Remove from the heat and return the scallops to the coconut cream mixture. Leave to cool for 5 minutes.

3 To serve, put equal amounts of the vermicelli noodles in bowls, spoon over the chicken, scallops and sauce and decorate with the coriander leaves.

TIP

To reconstitute the vermicelli noodles, put them in a bowl and cover with boiling water. Agitate in the bowl, then let them soak for 7–8 minutes. Drain and serve immediately.

smoked chicken, gnocchi and zucchini

SERVES 4

1 tablespoon extra-virgin olive oil

150 g zucchini, trimmed and finely
   sliced

2 tablespoons minced garlic

250 g smoked chicken meat, roughly
   chopped

400 g blanched gnocchi (see Basics
   page 135)

$1/2$ cup (125 ml) chicken stock
   (see Basics page 130)

$1/2$ cup (125 ml) white wine

$1/2$ cup (125 ml) cream

1 teaspoon salt

$1/4$ teaspoon cayenne pepper

1 Heat the oil in a large frying pan over medium heat and add the
   zucchini slices. Cook for 1 minute, then add the garlic and cook
   for 30 seconds.

2 Toss in the chicken and gnocchi; pour in the stock, wine and
   cream and bring to the boil. Reduce to a simmer and cook a
   further 4–5 minutes.

3 Season with salt and cayenne pepper and serve immediately
   with a good salad and garlic bread.

pork medallions, *aniseed carrots, apple and ginger sauce*

1 Flatten each round of pork by placing the pieces between plastic wrap and pounding gently with a meat mallet. Ensure all medallions are the same thickness.

2 Heat the oil and butter in a large frying pan and, when foaming, cook the pork until nearly done. Turn only once and do not overcook. Lift the meat from the pan and keep warm.

3 Add the onion to the frying pan and cook until softened and browned. Pour in the wine and add the tarragon, salt and pepper. Swirl in the pan to combine the flavours. Return the pork and its juices to the pan and move the pork around to reheat and combine all the ingredients.

4 Put the extra butter in another frying pan and place on medium heat. When melted, add the carrots and aniseed and toss to heat.

5 To serve, spoon equal amounts of carrots onto the side of the plates, sit the pork beside them and spoon over the pan juices. The apple and ginger sauce can be spooned over the pork or served separately. A dressed green salad sets this off.

SERVES 4

800 g pork fillet, trimmed and cut
  into 8 rounds

1 tablespoon light olive oil

1 tablespoon butter

1 small onion, finely chopped

$1/2$ cup (125 ml) dry white wine

1 tablespoon fresh tarragon
  (or 2 teapoons if dried)

$1/2$ teaspoon salt

$1/4$ teaspoon ground white pepper

1 tablespoon butter, extra

400 g diced carrots, blanched

$1/2$ teaspoon aniseed

apple and ginger sauce (see Basics
  page 133)

homemade *char seiu* and hokkien noodles

SERVES 4

for the char seiu

500 g pork fillet

2 tablespoons white sugar

$1/4$ teaspoon salt

3 tablespoons light soy sauce

2 tablespoons soybean paste

drop of red food colouring (optional)

for the noodles

1 tablespoon peanut oil

1 medium-sized onion, cut into
  8–10 wedges

2 medium-sized carrots, peeled and
  finely sliced on the diagonal

6 baby bok choy, washed, leaves cut
  from stems

$1/2$ cup (125 ml) chicken stock
  (see Basics page 130) or water

2 tablespoons kecap manis

400 g hokkien noodles, soaked in hot
  water to separate strands

fresh coriander leaves, for garnishing

You will see this delicious meat hanging up in the windows of Chinese barbecue restaurants. The Chinese do not always use fillets of pork, but for me, at home, this cut of meat is the best. I love char seiu and mostly make it without the superfluous colouring.

PREHEAT OVEN TO 190°C

1 Prepare the pork for marinating by trimming off all the fat and removing the 'silver'. In a large bowl, combine the sugar, salt, soy sauce, soybean paste and colouring (if you're using it). Mix well. Put in the pork and coat with the marinade. Leave to sit for 45–60 minutes.

2 Lift the fillets out of the marinade and place onto a cooking rack in a roasting pan. Roast in the oven for 15 minutes and then turn to cook another 15 minutes, or until the pork is cooked through. You can baste the fillets with the remaining marinade if you like, but it is not necessary. Remove from the oven, cover loosely with aluminium foil and cool, for at least 2 hours, before slicing.

3 When you are ready to serve, bring the peanut oil to smoking point in a wok and cook the onion and carrots for 1 minute. Take the bok choy and cut the white part into quarters, lengthwise. Add to the wok and stir in.

4 Pour in the stock or water, together with the kecap manis, and cook quickly for 1 minute. Add the sliced pork, stir well and then tip in the noodles and the retained bok choy leaves. Lift and heat the noodles through. When hot, tip into a large serving bowl and decorate with torn coriander leaves.

barbecuing
and grilling

simple but scrumptious

Barbecuing is enjoying a renaissance—not in my home, where it has always been a part of the cooking scene, but around the country. This style of cooking meat produces unique flavours that are irresistible. More so now than ever, the social activity surrounding the barbecue is what we busy people crave. Not only does the cooking and eating get done but we socialise with our friends and family at the same time.

Grilling, which I refer to as putting ingredients under a heat source, has its own way of imparting flavour and is a versatile way of preparing dishes for the table.

Once fashionable was the 'day-long marination' in preparation for cooking with these methods. These days we tend to prefer to let the natural flavours of the meat be enhanced by a short marinating process. The fact that our basic produce is so much better than it used to be also negates the need to use marinating as a tenderising process.

Memories of barbecues I have cooked all over the world are fond ones. Once, beside a centuries-old church outside Barcelona in Spain, we dined on my barbecue fare with locals, drinking wine from one of those squeezed goatskin bags. I ended up with wine all down my shirtfront! Another barbecue of note for me was cooking a whole pike on an open-fire barbie on the Isle of Wight—simple but scrumptious. But perhaps my best memories of barbecues are of my father's efforts on the old ploughshare over the 44-gallon drum. I'm reminded of how good food is, and of how bonding the barbie can be.

tips for barbecuing and grilling

- Always have the barbecue or grill preheated to the desired temperature.
- There are more temperature zones than 'nothing' and 'full on'. Remember, the meat needs to cook through, so a moderate temperature is necessary.
- Both barbecues and grill can be dangerous to children—please pay special attention to safety.
- Watch for cross-contamination. It is so easy to put cooked meat back onto a plate/platter that has had the raw stuff there. This is very dangerous and can cause illness.
- Having all the necessary equipment on hand for cooking is as essential here as it is elsewhere. Be prepared and have everything at hand.
- Use spray oil when cooking on a grill or barbecue. This way you get the flavour you need but you use less oil.
- Make sure you clean the grill and the barbie after each use.

IDEAL MEAT CUTS FOR BARBECUING AND GRILLING

LAMB	BEEF	VEAL	POULTRY	PORK
Chump chops	Rump steak	Chops	Duck breast fillets	Tenderloin
Cutlets	Scotch fillet	Tenderloin	Turkey steaks	Spare ribs (belly)
Leg chops	Tenderloin	Schnitzels	Chicken breast fillets	Spare ribs (babyback)
Loin chops	T-bone		Chicken Maryland	Boneless loin
Boneless loin	Striploin (sirloin)		Chicken thigh fillets	
Sausages	Sausages			
Racks	Hamburger mince			

barbecued *sirloin steak* with confit garlic butter

SERVES 4

4 x 250 g sirloin steaks, preferably
  5 cm thick and marbled

for the butter

250 g butter, at room temperature
8 confited garlic cloves, peeled
  (see Basics page 134)
1 tablespoon chopped fresh thyme
1 tablespoon red wine vinegar
1 tablespoon finely grated lemon zest

PREHEAT BARBECUE TO HOT

1 Trim the steaks of all fat that you don't want (leaving some on is a source of great flavour). Grind over with black pepper and set to one side.

2 Make the butter, which is better done the night before use. In a mixing bowl, mash all the ingredients together with a potato masher and then whisk to combine. The finished butter can then be placed in a serving bowl and refrigerated until ready for use. Alternatively, it can be rolled in greaseproof paper to a sausage shape and frozen.

3 Cook the steak on the open slat section of your very hot barbecue. Leave for 2 minutes, then flip onto another part of the barbecue where no meat has rested. (The reason for this is that the heat will have gone from the place where you've just cooked, and you need high heat to seal the meat.) Cook a further 2 minutes, then turn onto a spot that has medium heat and cook for 3 minutes on each side if you like your steak cooked to medium. For rare, cook the steaks for the initial 2 minutes on each side and then a further 1 minute on each side; for well done, cook for the initial 2 minutes on each side and then a further 5 minutes on each side. Lift the cooked meat onto a warmed plate and leave to sit for 3 minutes.

4 Serve on individual plates with the butter either served on the side in a bowl with a spoon (remove from the refrigerator 20 minutes before use), or cut into 1 cm thick rings if using the freezer method. The butter is delicious as it melts over the steak. Serve with barbecued sliced potatoes and a green salad.

char-grilled beef and peanut green curry

750 g sirloin plate, in one piece, all
fat and connective tissue removed

1/2 cup (125 ml) coconut milk

1/2 cup (125 ml) peanut green curry
paste (see Basics page 138)

1/2 cup unsalted roasted peanuts,
no skins and roughly chopped

2 cups (500 ml) coconut cream

1 tablespoon raw sugar (or palm
sugar if available)

1 teaspoon salt or fish sauce

3 long green chillies, seeded and cut
into fine strips

3 kaffir lime leaves, vein removed
and cut into fine strips

fresh coriander leaves

PREHEAT BARBECUE TO MEDIUM

1 Char-grill the beef for 5–7 minutes on each side, or until cooked to
medium; this will depend on the thickness of the beef. Remove and
let sit in a warm place for 15 minutes.

2 Bring the coconut milk to the boil in a wok and cook for 1 minute,
then add the peanut green curry paste and stir for 1 minute.
The liquid will become very fragrant.

3 Add two-thirds of the peanuts and the coconut cream. Cook until
heated through. Add the sugar and salt or fish sauce and stir in.
The liquid should now be heated, salty and sweet, so adjust the
flavours to your liking.

4 Add the chillies and kaffir lime leaves, remove from the heat and
stir for 1 minute.

5 Thinly slice the beef and place in a shallow bowl. Pour the curry
sauce on top, tear up the coriander leaves and sprinkle them over
the beef and sauce. Sprinkle with the remaining peanuts and serve
with cooked rice vermicelli noodles or steamed fragrant rice.

herb-infused crumbed *lamb cutlets* with vegetable compote and aioli

PREHEAT GRILL OR BARBECUE TO MEDIUM

1 Trim the lamb cutlets and sprinkle them with the combined parsley, oregano, mint, dill, lemon zest and pepper. Pat the mixture into the meat and leave to sit for 20 minutes.

2 Cook the cutlets until done to your liking. For rare, cook the cutlets for approximately 2 minutes on each side; for medium, cook for approximately 3 minutes on each side; for well done, cook for approximately 4 minutes on each side.

3 Meanwhile, heat the oil to medium in a large frying pan and tip in the mixed cooked vegetables. Toss, sprinkle with salt if you like and add the peas at the end of the cooking. Fry the vegetables until browned, or crisped if you prefer.

4 Serve the vegetables onto individual plates and arrange the cooked lamb cutlets against them. Spoon the aioli over the top and serve immediately.

SERVES 4

12 lamb cutlets

1 teaspoon each of finely chopped fresh parsley, oregano, mint and dill

1 teaspoon very finely grated lemon zest

$1/4$ teaspoon ground white pepper

1 tablespoon olive oil

2 cups roughly diced cooked vegetables, either baked or steamed, to include potatoes, carrots, pumpkin, celery and parsnip

$1/4$ cup frozen green peas

$1/2$ cup poached garlic aioli (see Basics page 134)

lamb cutlets with roasted beetroots and sauce paloise

SERVES 4

12 lamb cutlets

4 beetroots, tennis ball-sized

for the sauce

1 tablespoon finely chopped
  eschalots

2 tablespoons chopped fresh mint

1 tablespoon chopped fresh chervil

1 small sprig fresh thyme

2 tablespoons white vinegar

2 tablespoons white wine

2 egg yolks

120 g firm butter, cut into cubes

$1/2$ teaspoon lemon juice

cayenne pepper, to taste

1 tablespoon each of torn or chopped
  fresh mint and chervil

PREHEAT OVEN TO 180°C
PREHEAT BARBECUE OR GRILL TO MEDIUM

1 Take the cutlets from the refrigerator 30 minutes before use to bring to room temperature. Trim and sprinkle with ground black pepper.

2 Wash the beetroots and trim the tops right back, but not through the skin. Wrap in aluminium foil (shiny side against the beetroot) and cook in the oven for 1 hour. Test to see if cooked by inserting a skewer through the foil; if evenly cooked, the flesh will be soft. If not done, cook further. When cooked, remove from the oven and allow to cool.

3 Meanwhile, make the sauce by putting the eschalots, mint, chervil, thyme, vinegar and wine in a saucepan and boiling down by two-thirds. Remove from the heat and tip into the top of a double boiler. Cool for 2 minutes, add the egg yolks and whisk. Put over the top of simmering water and whisk until the mixture thickens. As it does, whisk in the butter until all is used. Remove from the heat, pour in the lemon and add salt and cayenne pepper to taste. Strain and stir in the mint and chervil.

4 Cook the lamb cutlets on a barbecue or grill until done to your liking. For rare, cook the cutlets for approximately 2 minutes on each side; for medium, cook for approximately 3 minutes on each side; for well done, cook for approximately 4 minutes each side.

5 Peel the cooled beetroots by rubbing the skin with the foil—the skin should lift off easily. Cut into halves or quarters. Serve the beetroot pieces in the centre of the individual plates and lean the cutlets against them. Serve the sauce separately and with a bowl of buttered cooked peas.

grilled *lamb loin chops* with olive and lemon pesto

SERVES 4

8–12 single lamb loin chops

3 tablespoons finely chopped fresh oregano

for the pesto

20 green olives, seeds removed

grated zest and juice of 1 lemon

3 cloves garlic, peeled and halved

1 tablespoon pine nuts

1 cup fresh flat-leaf (Italian) parsley leaves, washed

2 teaspoons grated Parmesan cheese

$1/3$ cup extra-virgin olive oil

500 g roasting potatoes

olive oil, for roasting

fresh rosemary sprigs

PREHEAT OVEN TO 200°C
PREHEAT GRILL TO MEDIUM

1 Trim the lamb chops if necessary and sprinkle both sides with the oregano. Press it into the meat, cover with plastic wrap and refrigerate for 1 hour.

2 To make the pesto, put the olives, lemon zest and juice, garlic, pine nuts, parsley and Parmesan cheese into a food processor bowl and start the motor. Gradually pour the extra-virgin olive oil down the feeder tube and work until combined. Remove the mixture from the processor bowl and store in a sterilised, airtight jar if you do not intend to use all the pesto at one time.

3 Wash the potatoes and peel if desired. Cut into bite-sized pieces and boil in water for 3 minutes. Heat a little oil in a roasting pan. When the potatoes are ready, drain them and let them sit to dry for 2 minutes, then carefully spoon them into the hot oil. Strip lots of leaves from the sprigs of rosemary and sprinkle them over the potatoes. Add salt and pepper to taste and bake in the oven until crisp and browned. Turn the potatoes regularly so they don't stick to the pan, and also to evenly coat with rosemary.

4 Grill the chops until done to your liking. For rare, cook the chops for approximately 3 minutes on each side; for medium cook for approximately 4 minutes on each side; for well done, cook for approximately 5 minutes each side.

5 Serve the chops on a bed of potatoes with the olive and lemon pesto on top of the chops. A dressed green salad with good Italian bread is all that is needed to finish this dish.

lamb burgers *with minted yoghurt and mint pesto*

PREHEAT GRILL OR BARBECUE TO MEDIUM

1 Cut the bread rolls in half and pull out the centre of each half so you have a well in each piece. Break the bread that you have removed into really small pieces and add to it the mince, eggs, sauces, onion, oil and salt. Mix well, using your hands. (The bread that you have used should be enough to be the binder. However, if your mixture is too moist, add enough dried breadcrumbs to take up that excess liquid.)

2 Shape the mince mixture into four patties of equal size. Cover and refrigerate for at least 1 hour.

3 Spray the patties with oil and cook on a barbecue or electric grill, or in a frying pan, over medium heat until just cooked. Turn only once or twice. When well done the juices coming out on top should be clear.

4 Spoon minted yoghurt into the well of each bread roll base and top with lettuce and a cooked patty. Smear with mint pesto and spoon over a little more yoghurt. Add the bread roll lids and press down to compress the fillings and make the burgers easier to eat.

4 large bread rolls

500 g lean lamb mince

2 eggs

1 teaspoon sweet chilli sauce

1 tablespoon Worcestershire sauce

1 small onion, finely diced

1 tablespoon extra-virgin olive oil

$1/2$ teaspoon salt

olive oil spray

300 g plain yoghurt mixed with $1/2$ cup freshly chopped mint

2 cups shredded iceberg lettuce, washed

mint pesto (see Basics page 136)

marjoram and cider vinegar
chicken cutlets

SERVES **4**

8 chicken cutlets

1 small green chilli, seeded and
finely chopped

3 tablespoons finely chopped fresh
marjoram

1 teaspoon ground coriander

1 tablespoon cider vinegar

2 tablespoons olive oil

$1/2$ teaspoon ground white pepper

PREHEAT BARBECUE TO MEDIUM—HOT

1 Put the chicken cutlets on a glass or ceramic plate and smear
with the chilli, marjoram and coriander. Massage in, then sprinkle
with the vinegar and oil. Move the cutlets around so they are well
coated, and refrigerate for 1 hour.

2 When ready to cook, drain the chicken cutlets and cook on the
barbecue. They will need approximately 3—4 minutes each side,
depending on the thickness of the meat. It is important that the
cutlets are cooked through. Sprinkle with white pepper and salt
as you cook.

3 When done, serve immediately with potato salad and a dressed
green salad.

chicken breast 'saltimbocca'

SERVES 4

4 single chicken breast fillets,
  or 2 double breast fillets cut in half
vegetable oil, for cooking
4 good slices ham, cut in half
  (or enough to cover the chicken)
8 fresh sage leaves
4 slices mozzarella cheese
  (or enough to cover the chicken)

PREHEAT GRILL TO HOT

1 Put the chicken breasts between layers of plastic wrap and pound gently with a meat mallet until of even thickness. Set to one side.

2 Over medium heat, seal each breast in an oiled frying pan until lightly browned on each side; do not cook through, as you have another cooking process to do yet and overcooking will dry out the meat. When browned, remove from the heat and allow to cool.

3 Place the cooled breasts on a flat tray or grilling tray. Cover with the slices of ham. Put two sage leaves on each breast and cover with cheese.

4 Grill until the cheese melts and browns. Serve with mixed vegetables or a salad of your choice.

grilled pork, apple and caraway burgers

1 Mix all the ingredients, except for the breadcrumbs and oil, in a large bowl. Use your hands for the best results. When combined, allow to sit for 30 minutes.

2 Shape the meat mixture into eight equal-sized patties and roll in the breadcrumbs. Place on a grilling tray.

3 Spray a little oil over the patties and cook, on both sides, until the juices run clear and the burgers are done.

4 Serve with salad and mustard of your choice.

SERVES 4

750 g pork mince

$1/2$ cup almond meal

1 large green apple, cored and finely diced

2 tablespoons chopped fresh flat-leaf (Italian) parsley leaves

1 teaspoon ground caraway seeds

2 eggs, lightly beaten

2 tablespoons plain flour

1 cup fresh breadcrumbs

vegetable oil spray

barbecued *pork chops* and mango mint sauce

SERVES 4

4 pork chops/cutlets

olive oil, for drizzling

1 large mango or two medium-sized
 mangoes

$1/2$ cup (125 ml) olive oil, extra

1 small green chilli, seeded and
 roughly chopped

$1/2$ teaspoon ground cumin

6 sprigs fresh mint, leaves only

cayenne pepper, to taste

As a Queenslander, I could eat a mango before I could crawl—well, nearly anyway! Mangoes are heavenly and for me always signal summer days sitting by the beach sucking on the sticky fruit, then into the cool water…

PREHEAT BARBECUE TO MEDIUM

1 Put the chops in a glass or ceramic bowl, drizzle over some olive oil and sprinkle on cracked black pepper to taste. Leave to sit for 30 minutes.

2 Remove the flesh from the mango by firstly cutting the cheeks from each side of the seed. Score the flesh, being careful not to cut through the skin. Scoop out the flesh using a dessertspoon and put in a food processor or blender. Add the extra oil, chilli, cumin and mint leaves, breaking the leaves up as you put them in the blender. Process to a smooth consistency and add salt and cayenne pepper to taste. Tip into a glass storage container.

3 Drain the chops and barbecue until done. Allow 4–6 minutes each side for thick chops and 3–5 minutes each side for thinner chops.

4 Serve with the mango sauce and salad of your choice.

braises and
casseroles

add a good stock and wait

Braising, casseroling, stewing—all are the essence of what cooking is about: the extraction of maximum flavour while tenderising a lesser cut of meat. Using a liquid and plenty of cooking time, all flavours are melded and converted into 'delicious'.

While braises and casseroles normally get shunted into the autumn and winter months of the year, a good stew will always be welcome in my home. Why? Well, it signifies that somebody took the time to cook. I mean really cook.

Braises and casseroles are often labelled 'comfort foods', which indeed they are. Did you ever have anything like your mother's steak and kidney pie? I can still taste my mum's version of Irish stew. These dishes represent a time when you felt secure, safe. For me they are weekend meals, which I can cook, cool and then place in the freezer for consumption later in the week.

Allow time for this type of cooking to happen. This is not 'add water and see'— this is add a good stock and wait. You will be rewarded, time and time again.

tips for braises and casseroles

- Always use a good stock and the appropriate one—beef with beef dishes, and so on.
- Make sure the meat you use is suitable (refer to the cuts chart below) and that it is cut into equal-sized pieces to ensure even cooking.
- Select a braising or casserole dish with a lid. So much of this type of cooking is done with the lid on to stop evaporation.
- Some fat and connective tissue can be left on the meat you use, as in the slow-cooking process these will almost always melt and add a lovely gelatinous consistency to the dish. Any fat that is rendered during the cooking can be scooped off or, better still, left overnight for the fat to settle on top and then removed.

IDEAL CUTS FOR BRAISES AND CASSEROLES

LAMB	BEEF	VEAL	POULTRY	PORK
Corned leg	Chuck steak	Legs	Big ducks	Pumped leg
Chump chops	Round steak	Stuffed breasts	Turkey hindquarter	Diced forequarter
Leg chops	Brisket	Rolled shoulders	Bigger, older chickens	Whole chump
Shoulder	Corned meats	Shin meat—osso buco	Chicken thigh cutlets	Diced leg meat
Best neck chops	Shin meat		Chicken Maryland	Sausages
Shanks	Sausages		Chicken legs	Neck
Chump chops	Chuck tender			

veal rolls in ginger tomato sauce

for the filling

200 g veal mince

1 tablespoon finely chopped
  green onions

1 clove garlic, minced

1 tablespoon finely chopped
  crystallised ginger

1 egg

$^1/_4$–$^1/_2$ cup dry breadcrumbs

4 x 100–120 g flattened veal steaks

3–4 tablespoons plain flour

1 tablespoon butter

1 medium-sized onion, roughly
  chopped

1 medium-sized carrot, roughly diced

$^1/_2$ cup diced celery

2 cups (500 ml) pasta tomato sauce

3 cups (750 ml) beef stock
  (see Basics page 131)

$^1/_2$ cup chopped crystallised ginger

This dish had a very good reception when I cooked it live on German TV in Baden Baden. The whole experience was quite remarkable, as there were two rehearsals to ensure the timing was correct to fit in with a very tight schedule. What made it so interesting was that I don't speak German and there was very little English spoken on the set! It was another example, to me, that food speaks all languages.

PREHEAT OVEN TO 180°C

1 Combine the mince, green onions, garlic, crystallised ginger, egg and salt and pepper to taste. Mix well and use enough breadcrumbs to take up any extra moisture.

2 Lay the four veal steaks out flat and top with equal quantities of the seasoned veal mince. Roll and secure with toothpicks. Dust the rolls with flour.

3 On the stove top, melt the butter, on medium heat, in a suitable-sized ovenproof roasting pan (with lid). Add the onion, carrot and celery and cook for 2 minutes. Add the floured veal rolls and lightly brown.

4 Pour in the tomato sauce and the stock. Bring to the boil. Transfer to the oven and cook for 1 hour, or until done.

5 Remove from the oven, season with the extra ginger, plus salt and pepper to taste. Serve with cooked rissoni pasta and green vegetables.

braised *veal tongues* and cumberland sauce

2 small to medium-sized veal
 tongues

1 onion, roughly chopped

1 tomato, roughly chopped

1 carrot, peeled and roughly chopped

1 stick celery, roughly chopped

$1/4$ cup (60 ml) white vinegar

2 cardamom pods

$1/2$ teaspoon caraway seeds

cumberland sauce

  (see Basics page 132)

PREHEAT OVEN TO 180°C

1 Wash the tongues and dry them with kitchen towels. Pull them into a round shape and skewer into place satay sticks. This allows for even cooking.

2 Into a braising pot put the onion, tomato, carrot and celery. Sit the tongues on top and add the vinegar and enough water to cover. Put in the cardamom pods and caraway seeds and bring to the boil on the stove top. Cover, transfer to the oven and continue cooking for 45 minutes.

3 Test to see if the meat is cooked by inserting a metal skewer into the thickest part of the tongues. When the juices run clear, they are ready. Remove from the oven and allow to cool slightly.

4 Lift the tongues from the cooking liquid. Remove the skewers and peel off the white layer of the tongues. Do this by using the tip of a paring knife just slipped under the layer: press down onto the tip of the paring knife with your thumb and then pull away from the meat—it will peel like an orange. Return the stripped tongue to the cooking liquid and allow to cool completely.

5 To serve, drain, then slice the tongue thinly and serve with dressed salads of your choice and with Cumberland sauce on the side.

corned *leg of lamb* with tomato relish

This is one of the all-time best meat dishes—we used to have it as children. The mutton was pumped with a brine and allowed to sit to 'corn' in it. Sometimes called poor-man's ham, corned lamb is wonderful both hot and cold. The relish is a quickie. Again, it can be served either hot or cold.

1 Put the bay leaves, peppercorns, cardamom pods, mustard seeds, mustard powder, vinegar and sugar in a large boiling pot. Top with water and then immerse the leg of lamb into it. (Ensure the lamb is covered by at least 6 cm of water.) Bring to the boil and then simmer until the lamb is cooked—allow 20 minutes per 500 g.

2 Approximately 45 minutes before the leg is cooked, add the potatoes, onions and carrots and cook until both the vegetables and meat are done. The vegetables must not be mushy and collapsing.

3 Remove the whole pot from the heat and lift out the meat to rest. Lift out the vegetables with a slotted spoon and keep hot. (If you are not serving the lamb immediately, it is better to leave the meat to cool in the cooking water. Remove the vegetables.)

4 To serve, slice the meat and pile the slices on plates beside the vegetables. Serve the tomato relish on the side, along with steamed green vegetables of your choice.

SERVES 4–6

3 bay leaves

1 tablespoon black peppercorns

2 cardamom pods

1 tablespoon mustard seeds

1 tablespoon dried mustard powder

$1/2$ cup (125 ml) white vinegar

2 tablespoons brown sugar

1 corned leg of lamb (pumped leg)

4 medium-sized potatoes, Desiree if possible

4 medium-sized onions, peeled

4 medium-sized carrots, peeled

tomato relish (see Basics page 132)

braised *lamb shanks* with white bean purée

SERVES 4

4 large or 8 small lamb shanks

2 tablespoons olive oil

1 large onion, roughly chopped

2 medium-sized carrots, peeled and
  roughly diced

2 sticks celery, roughly chopped

4 cloves garlic, crushed

4 cups (1 L) lamb or beef stock
  (see Basics page 131), or enough
  to cover the ingredients well

3 bay leaves

500 g cannellini beans, soaked in
  water overnight

400 g canned tomatoes

Lamb shanks have taken on a whole new status in the cooking world: they have gone from being regarded as dogs' meat to being a gourmet product in very quick time. These shanks are simple yet delectable, and the white bean purée takes the place of potato mash beautifully.

PREHEAT OVEN TO 180°C

1 Seal the lamb shanks by pan-frying either in a dry pan or in the casserole dish itself.

2 In a flameproof casserole, heat the oil and brown the onion, carrots, celery and garlic. Lay the shanks in, pour in the stock and bring to a simmer. Add the bay leaves.

3 Tip the cannellini beans onto a muslin cloth and tie to secure. Put them in with the shanks, cover and place in the oven.

4 After 1 hour, check to see that the beans are cooked. When done, remove from the casserole, along with 1 cup (250 ml) of the cooking liquid. Add the tomatoes to the casserole dish and continue cooking in the oven for up to another 1 hour, or until the meat is tender and coming away from the bone.

5 Purée the beans in a food processor with enough of the cooking liquid to make a paste. Season with salt and white pepper and store in a warm place or in a microwave-safe container.

6 When the shanks are ready, check the seasoning and remove the bay leaves. Spoon some of the reheated bean purée into the centre of the plates and put shanks on top. Ladle some of the cooking juices around and over the shanks and serve with cooked green vegetables or a ratatouille.

steak and kidney

SERVES 4–6

750 g chuck steak, cut into 3 cm
thick slices

200 g beef kidney, trimmed and cut
into 2 cm thick slices

plain flour, for coating

1 large onion, roughly chopped

1 medium-sized carrot, roughly
chopped

2–3 cups (500–750 ml) veal or beef
stock (see Basics page 131)

1 tablespoon Worcestershire sauce

3 large potatoes, skins on and cut
into large dice

Mums have been great inspirations to all cooks—and reading Stephanie Alexander's wonderful *The Cook's Companion* I notice her mum's steak and kidney is featured. Well, here is my version of my mum's. It can be easily turned into a pie.

1 Cut the steak into 3 cm cubes and roll them and the kidney slices in the flour. Put them on top of the onion and carrot in a large, heavy-based saucepan with a lid. Add the stock and Worcestershire sauce so that the meat is only just covered. Stir well.

2 Bring the mixture up to a simmer and cook for 90 minutes. Add the potatoes and cook for 1 hour.

3 Season with salt and pepper to taste. When the potatoes and meat are tender, serve with mashed peas or Brussels sprouts.

TIP

This solid, scrummy dish can easily be turned into a pie using the same pastry and method used in the veal and fragrant vegetable pie (see page 120).

beef *and herb curry*

I saw a recipe, similar to this, cooked by an Indian lady chef when I was filming for the 'Today' show in Fiji. I was amazed by its simplicity and its alluring flavours.

1 In a large metal pot, heat the oil and, when smoking, tip in the mustard seeds. Cover with a lid and leave to sit for 15 seconds, then add the onion and cook for 1 minute, stirring all the time. Add the garlic, curry leaves and curry powder. Stir for 30 seconds and then add the beef pieces. Move around the pot to seal and coat the beef with the curry mixture.

2 Pour in the stock. Bring to a simmer and cook for 1 hour. (Check to see the beef is cooked through before serving, as stewing meat can take longer to cook than round or chuck steak.)

3 Sprinkle in equal amounts of the herbs, to taste. Stir in and cook for 5 minutes.

4 Serve the curry with heaps of cooked long-grain rice and suitable sambals, such as bananas sprinkled with desiccated coconut, chopped onions and tomatoes, mango chutney and natural yoghurt.

SERVES 4

2 tablespoons vegetable oil

1 tablespoon black mustard seeds

1 medium-sized onion, finely diced

2 cloves garlic, chopped

8 fresh curry leaves

2 tablespoons curry powder
  (see Basics page 138)

600 g beef (round, chuck or stewing
  meat), cut into bite-sized pieces

3 cups (750 ml) beef stock
  (see Basics page 131)

tarragon, parsley and chives,
  chopped

lamb-stuffed baby red onions

SERVES 6

2 cups (500 ml) chicken stock
(see Basics page 130) mixed
with 1 cup (250 ml) water
6 medium-sized red onions
250 g lamb mince
1/4 cup burghul wheat, soaked
overnight in water
2 tablespoons toasted pine nuts
1 tablespoon chopped fresh mint
1 small tomato, halved, seeded
and finely diced
1/4 teaspoon ground cumin
1/4 teaspoon ground turmeric

In my home town of Noosa Heads there are a multitude of good chefs. Leonie Palmer and Stef Fisher are amongst the best, and this recipe comes from their waterfront restaurant, Ricky Ricardo's. I have 'tweaked' it for us at home.

PREHEAT OVEN TO 170°C

1 Bring the chicken stock and water to the boil on the stove top. Add the onions, whole, and simmer for 10 minutes. Lift out to cool and retain the cooking liquid.

2 Mix the lamb mince, drained burghul, pine nuts, mint, tomato, cumin and turmeric together in a bowl. Season with salt and white pepper.

3 Trim the tops off the onions and gently remove the skins. With a small spoon, scoop out the centre of the onions, leaving the three outside layers intact. Retain the scooped-out flesh and then stuff the lamb mixture into the hollowed onions. Pile it up.

4 Dice the retained onion flesh and put it into a casserole or braising pan along with the stuffed onions. The onions must sit very snugly in this pan to ensure they remain sitting up. Tip 1 cup (250 ml) of the retained cooking liquid around the onions, cover with a lid and cook in the oven for 30 minutes.

5 Remove the dish from the oven and lift the stuffed onions out onto a serving platter. Purée the diced onion and cooking liquid in a food processor or blender. When done, check for seasoning and spoon over the top of the stuffed onions.

mum's *beef sausage* casserole

SERVES 4

2 medium-sized onions, cut into rings

1 carrot, peeled and diced

2 sticks celery, trimmed and diced

1 large parsnip, peeled, cored and
   diced

1 cup long-grain rice

8 good beef sausages, separated

beef stock, to cover (see Basics
   page 131)

2 bay leaves

2 tablespoons chopped fresh
   curly-leaf parsley

I love this recipe, as we grew up with it as children. Mum would make lashings of the casserole, and now I appreciate it as one-pot cooking at its best. She would put peas in at the last minute to cook them. Less washing up!

PREHEAT OVEN TO 180°C

1 In a large, flattish casserole dish, layer the onion, carrot, celery and parsnip. Sprinkle in the rice and put the sausages on top. Pour in enough stock to cover the sausages well, and top with the bay leaves.

2 Cook in the oven for 1 hour, stirring the ingredients twice in this time. You may need to season with salt if you like, but generally the sausages have a good amount of salt and white pepper in them.

3 Serve immediately, sprinkled with chopped parsley, with lots of cooked green vegetables.

red wine *chicken casserole* and zucchini bread

This Burgundian casserole was one of the first dishes I learnt to cook and it subsequently went onto all the menus in the restaurants I operated over the years. The dish has many variations. This is mine.

PREHEAT OVEN TO 180°C

1 Heat the butter and oil in a large flameproof casserole dish and, when foaming, brown the chicken thighs in two batches. Remove, keep warm and collect the juices.

2 Add the bacon pieces and onions to the casserole dish and cook for 3 minutes. Sprinkle in the flour and stir well, then pour in the red wine and stir until bubbling.

3 Add the garlic and return the chicken and juices to the casserole dish. Top with the majoram and thyme. Making sure the chicken is immersed, cover and cook for 30 minutes. Remove from the oven and add the mushrooms. Season with salt and pepper to taste, cover and return to cook for a further 15 minutes.

4 When cooked, serve with rice and zucchini bread, which can be pan-fried, toasted or grilled.

TIP

While red meat dishes are generally best left a day before consuming, dishes based on chicken are best consumed immediately they are done. While a day may improve the taste, the reheating process does nothing for appearances: chicken meat comes away from the bones and normally becomes stringy and unattractive.

SERVES 4

60 g butter

2 tablespoons olive oil

8 chicken thigh cutlets, patted dry with kitchen towels

100 g shoulder bacon, cut into rough dice

12 pickling or button onions, peeled

3 tablespoons plain flour

2 cups (500 ml) red wine

2 cloves garlic, roughly chopped

3 sprigs fresh majoram

2 sprigs fresh thyme

12 button mushrooms, stalks removed, wiped with a damp cloth

cooked long-grain rice

zucchini bread (see Basics page 133)

poached chicken *with marinated leeks and goat's curd*

4 cups (1 L) chicken stock
  (see Basics page 130)

$1/2$ cup (125 ml) white wine

10 fresh flat-leaf (Italian) parsley
  stems and leaves

4 x 150–200 g chicken breast fillets,
  trimmed of all fat

8 medium-sized leeks, white parts
  only, halved lengthwise and washed
  thoroughly

$1/4$ cup (60 ml) olive oil

1 tablespoon almond flakes

200 g goat's curd

for the marinade

$1/2$ cup (125 ml) extra-virgin olive oil

$1/2$ cup (125 ml) lemon juice

3 tablespoons raisins

Goat's curd and other goat's milk cheeses are really popular in Australia now. In France these products are seen everywhere, and with good reason—they're delicious.

PREHEAT OVEN TO 180°C

1 In a saucepan, bring the stock, wine and parsley stems (not leaves) to the boil and add the chicken breasts. Reduce to a simmer and poach for 15 minutes. Remove from the heat and let the chicken cool in the stock. When cooled, refrigerate ready for use.

2 Put the leeks into a baking dish and drizzle with the olive oil. Cover and cook in the oven until tender but still holding together—this will take 25–30 minutes, depending on the size of the leeks.

3 Mix the marinade ingredients while the leeks cook. Remove the leeks from the oven and spoon over the marinade. Chop or tear up the parsley leaves and scatter them over the leeks, then add the almond flakes. Leave to cool and turn the leeks carefully, at least twice.

4 To serve, place four leek halves into the centre of individual plates. Remove the cooled chicken from the stock and slice lengthwise into four long strips. Place across the top of the leeks and spoon on the goat's curd. Spoon the leek marinade over the top.

braised duck and *parsley lentils*

SERVES 4

1 x 1.7 kg duck, cavity wiped out
  and stuffed with thyme sprigs,
  bay leaves and parsley, to taste
2 medium-sized onions, peeled
  and sliced thinly
1 tablespoon brandy
1 cup (250 ml) port wine
800 ml chicken stock (see Basics
  page 130)
grated zest of 1 orange
200 g brown-green lentils, soaked
  in cold water for 2 hours
1/4 cup chopped fresh flat-leaf
  (Italian) parsley leaves
1 tablespoon butter (optional)

PREHEAT OVEN TO 180°C

1 Wipe the skin of the duck with kitchen towels. Put the onions into the
  base of a casserole dish and place the duck on top.

2 Heat the brandy in a small saucepan and ignite it, with a match,
  before pouring it over the duck. Bring the port wine and chicken stock
  to the boil and then pour it around the duck. Sprinkle the orange zest
  around the duck and place the casserole in the oven for 75 minutes,
  basting the duck every 20 minutes.

3 When done, remove the casserole from the oven and lift the duck out.
  Keep warm. While your doing this, return the remaining duck liquid to
  the stove top and simmer to reduce the quantity by a quarter. Remove
  2 cups (500 ml) of the cooking liquid from the casserole, combine
  with 1 cup (250 ml) of water and pour into a saucepan with the
  lentils and parsley. Simmer until all the liquid is absorbed—this will
  take around 5–8 minutes. The lentils must stay whole and firm (not
  crunchy).

4 Cut the duck into serving portions—generally quarters. Spoon the
  lentils onto plates and place the duck on top. You might like to add
  a tablespoon of butter to enrich the lentils just before you serve.
  Ladle over some of the reduced cooking liquid and serve with
  cooked silverbeet and other vegetables of your choice.

braised *pork sausages* and chick peas

When we filmed for the 'Today' show in Rhinegau in Germany, I was one of the Aussie chefs presenting Australian foods and wines. The Germans loved our foods, and me?—well, I fell in love with their sausages. This dish is similar to one I had in Frankfurt.

PREHEAT OVEN TO 180°C

1 Place the tomato sauce, stock, wine, chickpeas and eschalots in a large ovenproof saucepan or casserole dish. Bring to a simmer on the stove top and cook for 40 minutes.

2 Remove from the heat and stir in the parsnip and parsley. Add the sausages and immerse them in the chickpea mixture. Return to the heat with the lid on, either on top of the stove or in the oven. Cook for 30 minutes, then remove from the heat and allow to cool for 10 minutes.

3 Combine the breadcrumbs and cheese and sprinkle evenly over the top of the sausages.

4 Turn the oven up to 200°C and put the casserole in, without a lid. Cook until the top is browned and crisp. Serve with cooked green vegetables of your choice.

SERVES 4

2 cups (500 ml) pasta tomato sauce

$1/2$ cup (125 ml) chicken stock (see Basics page 130)

$1/2$ cup (125 ml) red wine

1 cup dried chickpeas, soaked overnight

2 eschalots, roughly chopped

1 large parsnip, peeled and roughly diced

$1/2$ cup chopped fresh flat-leaf (Italian) parsley leaves

8 medium-sized pork sausages, blanched

1 cup dried breadcrumbs

$1/2$ cup grated Romano cheese

braised *pork neck* 'tonnato'

1.5 kg pork neck

$^1\!/_2$ cup finely diced celery

$^1\!/_2$ cup finely diced onion

1 large sprig fresh rosemary

4–8 cups (1–2 L) chicken stock
  (see Basics page 130)

for the tonnato dressing

185 g canned tuna, drained

4 anchovy fillets

$1^1\!/_2$ cups mayonnaise

1 tablespoon white vinegar

$^1\!/_2$ teaspoon salt

$^1\!/_4$ teaspoon ground white pepper

fresh tarragon (optional)

8–12 capers

1 Trim the pork neck and tie it with string. The cut of meat is quite loose in structure and so will respond better to cooking when tied. You can always ask the butcher to do it for you.

2 Put the celery and onion in a large braising pot with a lid. Place the pork on top of the vegetables, then add the rosemary and enough chicken stock to cover the meat. Put the lid on and cook in the oven for 90 minutes. When done, remove from the oven and leave to cool in the cooking liquid. When cooled, refrigerate overnight.

3 Make the tonnato dressing by mixing all the dressing ingredients except the tarragon in a food processor and working to a paste. Tear up the tarragon leaves and stir them into the paste.

4 To serve, remove the pork from the liquid and drain. Cut into very fine slices and arrange them in an overlapping, circular fashion on a large plate. Spoon over the tonnato dressing and sprinkle on the capers. Serve with a celery, apple and pine nut salad and a dressed green salad.

roasts and
baked dishes

a real meal

Call me old-fashioned if you will, but to me a real meal is a roasted meal.

There are many reasons why I like roasting my meat. For one thing, if done properly, roasting can save time. Roasting can also be a means of 'one-pot cooking'—a popular concept these days—since it's a great way to meld the flavours of various ingredients.

But what is the difference between roasting and baking? Well, the word 'roasting' comes from the term 'spit-roasting', harking back to a time when the meat was revolved on a spit over a heat source. Baking, on the other hand, has always referred to what is cooked in the oven.

Of course, these days not too many homes have a spit, so roasting has come to be understood as a moist cooking method. During the cooking process, a crispy skin or crust forms, which keeps in the juices. Basting with the cooking juices on a regular basis enhances the flavour of the roast and also helps keep the moisture inside.

By contrast, baking is a dry cooking method and generally refers to cooking a pastry item. No basting is done. The old baked dinner, as we used to call it, should really have been called a roast dinner.

One of those lively discussions that foodies have, especially after a glass or two of red, is, 'Did cooking really start with roasting?' Some certainly think so, and from all I have read spit-roasting was probably there from the beginning. All I know is that using the oven is one of the very best ways to cook. For good even heat and surround heat, roasting or baking in the oven is fantastic.

roasting and baking tips

- Don't forget to preheat the oven to the desired temperature before use.
- Test your oven for accuracy—for older ovens I recommend buying an oven thermometer which will sit on, or hang from, the cooking racks.
- Use the timing given as a guide only. You will come to know your own oven and when your meat is cooked. Failing that, a meat thermometer, which is used to insert into the thickest part of a roast, is inexpensive and provides peace of mind if you have a tricky oven.
- Ensure the item to be cooked is at room temperature before putting it into the oven.
- Meat should be sealed before roasting. This can be done beforehand in hot oil on the stove top if you are using small cuts of meat. For large items such as a turkey, whole rump or a big leg of lamb, start off with the oven on very high, say 220°C. After 15 minutes turn it down to around 180°C or 200°C.
- Don't cook too many vegetables in the same roasting pan as the meat—you need room to turn the vegetables so they become crispy on the outside.
- When roasting meat on its own, put it on a rack with some water underneath. This keeps the meat out of the fat and the water stops the fat from spitting all over the oven.
- Always let your meat rest for a minimum of 10 minutes after it has been cooked, especially if it is well done. This process lets the meat juices set so they don't run when you carve. Large cuts or turkeys can be left for up to 30 minutes, as they will retain their heat.
- Use a thick-based roasting pan. This will enable you to prepare the gravy in the same pan on the stove top.

IDEAL CUTS FOR ROASTING

Before you begin, look at what cut you are considering roasting. Texture is always important to cooking times and to the choice of cooking method. For example, coarse cuts, like chuck steak, do not lend themselves to roasting, while finer-grained meats such as tenderloins are good but need to be tied into place to ensure even cooking.

LAMB	BEEF	VEAL	POULTRY	PORK
Leg, bone in	Point of rump	Leg	Whole chicken	Leg
Leg, boned and tied	Striploin (sirloin)	Tenderloin	Boned and rolled chicken	Boneless loin
Crown roast	Tenderloin	Boned and rolled shoulders	Chicken Maryland	Boned shoulder
Shoulder, bone in or boned and seasoned	Whole blade (slow-roasted)	Rack	Whole duck	Rack
Rack	Rib roast		Duck Maryland	
Saddle			Turkey buffe	
Boned loin			Whole turkey	

INTERNAL TEMPERATURE GAUGE

A meat thermometer inserted into the thickest part of a roast will help you gauge when the meat is done to your liking. Use the following temperatures as a guide.

medium rare to medium	55ºC–60ºC
medium to medium well	65ºC–70ºC
well done	75ºC–80ºC

roasting chart

The following times given are approximate and per 500 g.

	RARE	MEDIUM	WELL DONE
LAMB LEG	Temp 200°C Mins 15–18	Temp 200°C Mins 18–22	Temp 200°C Mins 25–28
	Cook at given temperatures for first 10 minutes, then 160°C for remainder of cooking time		
LAMB LEG (BONED)	Temp 220°C Mins 10–15	Temp 220°C Mins 15–18	Temp 200°C Mins 20–25
	Cook at given temperatures for first 10 minutes, then 180°C for remainder of cooking time		
LAMB LOIN (BONELESS)	Temp 220°C Mins 12–15	Temp 220°C Mins 15–20	Temp 200°C Mins 20–25
	Cook at given temperatures for first 10 minutes, then 180°C for remainder of cooking time		
LAMB SHOULDER	not applicable	Temp 200°C Mins 18–20	Temp 200°C Mins 20–25
RACK OF LAMB 7–8 CUTLETS	Temp 220°C Mins 15–17	Temp 200°C Mins 17–20	Temp 200°C Mins 20–25
BEEF FILLET (TENDERLOIN)	Temp 220°C Mins 12–15	Temp 220°C Mins 15–20	Temp 220°C Mins 20–25
	Cook at given temperatures for first 10 minutes, then 200°C for remainder of cooking time		
SCOTCH FILLET	Temp 200°C Mins 12–15	Temp 200°C Mins 15–20	Temp 200°C Mins 20–25
RUMP	Temp 200°C Mins 12–15	Temp 200°C Mins 15–20	Temp 200°C Mins 25–30
STRIPLOIN (SIRLOIN)	Temp 220°C Mins 12–15	Temp 220°C Mins 15–20	Temp 200°C Mins 25–30
RIB OF BEEF	Temp 220°C Mins 12–15	Temp 220°C Mins 15–20	Temp 200°C Mins 30–35
	Cook at given temperatures for first 10 minutes, then reduce by 20°C for remainder of cooking time		
VEAL LEG	Temp 180°C Mins 15–18	Temp 180°C Mins 18–22	not applicable
VEAL LOIN (BONELESS)	Temp 180°C Mins 20–25	Temp 180°C Mins 25–30	not applicable
WHOLE CHICKEN	not applicable	not applicable	Temp 200°C Mins 15–20
PORK LEG WITH CRACKLING	not applicable	Temp 230°C Mins 25–30	Temp 230°C Mins 30–35
	Cook at given temperatures for first 20 minutes, then 180°C for remainder of cooking time		
PORK RACK	not applicable	Temp 200°C Mins 25–30	Temp 200°C Mins 30–35
	Cook at given temperatures for first 10 minutes, then 180°C for remainder of cooking time		
PORK LOIN	not applicable	Temp 170°C Mins 30–32	Temp 170°C Mins 32–35

moroccan spice rub *lamb* and couscous compote

SERVES **4**

30 g ras el hanout spice rub

1.5 kg boneless leg of lamb

for the compote

1 tablespoon extra-virgin olive oil

1 tablespoon finely diced onion

500 g cooked Israeli couscous
  (boil for 10–15 minutes in water),
  kept warm

1 tablespoon shredded preserved
  lemon zest

3 tablespoons diced fresh tomato
  flesh

2 tablespoons lemon juice

$1/2$ cup chopped fresh mint

harissa paste (optional)

The spice rub used in this dish—ras el hanout—literally means 'top of the shelf', or the very best. Our lamb deserves the best, and this mix brings out the best in it. Israeli couscous is larger than normal couscous and so takes longer to cook. Both ras el hanout and Israeli couscous can be purchased from Middle-Eastern grocery shops.

PREHEAT OVEN TO 220°C (FOR RARE AND MEDIUM) OR 200°C (FOR WELL DONE)

1 Liberally rub the spice into both the cut and skin sides of the lamb, then roll and tie the leg of lamb into a long, cylindrical shape.

2 Place on a cooking rack in a roasting pan and cook in the oven for 10 minutes. Decrease the temperature to 180°C and cook until done. For rare, cook for approximately 30–45 minutes; for medium cook for 45–55 minutes; for well done cook for 60–75 minutes. Remove from the oven and leave to rest in a warm place for 10 minutes before carving.

3 While the lamb cooks, make the couscous compote. Heat the oil in a suitable-sized frying pan over medium heat and cook the onion for 1 minute. Tip in the cooked couscous, lemon zest, tomato and lemon juice and cook for 2–4 minutes, stirring constantly, until all the ingredients are heated through. When the lamb is ready to be sliced, add the chopped mint and stir through.

4 Spoon the couscous into the centre of the plates and layer slices of lamb over the top. Serve with steamed snow peas or a green vegetable of your choice, and the harissa paste on the side.

baked *racks of lamb* with honey and cumin baba ghanoush

SERVES 4

2 x 8 cutlet racks of lamb, trimmed

for the baba ghanoush

4 eggplants, around 300 g each,
  cut in half lengthways

vegetable oil, for brushing

5 cloves garlic

1 teaspoon salt

$1/2$ cup (125 ml) tahini

$1/4$ cup (60 ml) lemon juice

2 tablespoons honey, warmed

1 teaspoon ground cumin

**PREHEAT BARBECUE TO MEDIUM—HOT
PREHEAT OVEN TO 220°C (FOR RARE) OR
200°C (FOR MEDIUM AND WELL DONE)**

1 Place the racks of lamb on a cooking rack in a roasting pan. Sprinkle with salt and white pepper to taste. Leave to one side until the baba ghanoush is made.

2 Cut diamond slits into the cut side of the eggplant halves and brush with oil. Put the eggplants, flesh-side down, onto a medium—hot open barbecue and cook, turning regularly, for 30 minutes or until the flesh is soft and coming away from the skin. Remove from the heat and cool until able to handle.

3 Peel the skin away from the cooked eggplant flesh. Put the flesh in a food processor with the garlic, salt, tahini, lemon juice, honey and cumin. Process into a smooth paste, remove from the bowl and keep warm.

4 Cook the lamb racks in the oven until rare or medium. For rare, cook for approximately 15—17 minutes; for medium, cook for approximately 17—20 minutes; for well done cook for approximately 20—25 minutes. Remove from the oven and allow to sit for 10 minutes before serving.

5 Spoon the desired amount of baba ghanoush to one side of each plate. Divide each rack in half and place one half on each plate beside the baba ghanoush. Serve with steamed bok choy or green vegetables of your choice.

herb and mustard crusted leg of lamb

PREHEAT OVEN TO 200°C

1 Make sure the lamb is at room temperature before placing it on a cooking rack in a roasting pan. Brush with soy sauce and cook in the oven for 15 minutes.

2 Mix the breadcrumbs, garlic, mustard, parsley, thyme, ginger and wine to make a rough, crumbly paste—more wine may be needed. Add salt and pepper, if desired.

3 Lift the lamb out of the oven and allow to cool for 15–20 minutes. Spoon and press the breadcrumb mixture over the lamb. Reduce the oven temperature to 160°C and return the lamb to cook until done to your liking. For rare, cook for approximately 60–80 minutes; for medium, cook for 75–90 minutes; for well done cook for 100–110 minutes.

4 When the crust is crisp and brown, remove the lamb from the oven and leave to sit for 10 minutes before carving. Serve with vegetables and a little dressed salad.

TIP

Note that the lamb is cooked at a low heat for this recipe because of the crust, which will discolour badly if cooked at a higher temperature. Baste the lamb every 20 minutes or so to get the most out of the juices it produces.

SERVES 4–6

2 kg leg of lamb, bone in

1 tablespoon soy sauce

1 cup dried breadcrumbs

1 clove garlic, finely minced

1 tablespoon smooth French mustard

1 tablespoon finely chopped fresh curly-leaf parsley

1 tablespoon finely chopped fresh thyme

$1/2$ teaspoon dried ground ginger

1 tablespoon white wine

star anise rack of lamb with dried peach relish

SERVES 4

2 x 8 cutlet racks of lamb,
  trimmed

$1/2$ cup (125 ml) kecap manis

4 star anise

$1/2$ cup (125 ml) mirin

$1/4$ cup raw sugar

for the relish (makes 3–4 cups)

300 g dried peaches, roughly
  chopped

90 g raw sugar

10 juniper berries

1 cup (250 ml) white vinegar

2 teaspoons grated orange zest

1 teaspoon ground cardamom

$1/2$ teaspoon ground cumin

$1/4$ teaspoon ground coriander

1 teaspoon salt

$1/2$ cup (125 ml) port wine

PREHEAT OVEN TO 220°C (FOR RARE) OR 200°C (FOR MEDIUM AND WELL DONE)

1 Leave the lamb racks to come to room temperature before cooking. Put the kecap manis, star anise, mirin, sugar and $1/2$ cup (125 ml) of water in a saucepan and bring to the boil. Simmer for 20 minutes, then remove from the heat.

2 Make the relish by covering the peaches with boiling water and leaving them to soak for 30 minutes. Strain and reserve half the liquid. Combine this reserved liquid with the remaining relish ingredients, except for the salt, and simmer for 45 minutes, stirring constantly. Add salt for the last 5 minutes of cooking. Remove from the heat and cool. To keep, store in sterilised jars.

3 Place the lamb on a cooking rack in a roasting pan and brush liberally with the kecap manis mixture. Place in the oven and cook until done. For rare, cook for approximately 15–17 minutes; for medium, cook for approximately 17–20 minutes; for well done, cook for approximately 20–25 minutes. Baste the lamb with the kecap manis mixture at least once during the cooking.

4 Remove from the oven, lift out the lamb and leave to sit for 10 minutes before carving, or serve a rack of 4 cutlets per person if you prefer.

5 Drain any excess fat from the roasting pan and put over high heat on the stove top. When the sediment starts to crackle, pour in the port wine and stir to incorporate. Spoon over each rack and serve with the relish to one side, and roasted vegetables of your choice.

sumac-dusted *leg of lamb* with garlic and red wine sauce

One of the great pleasures in my career has been cooking Australian lamb all over the world. It is a superb product and one which I never tire of using. Sumac spice is relatively new to us in Australia but it has been known for centuries in the Middle East. It is a natural partner for lamb.

PREHEAT OVEN TO 200°C

1 With a sharp knife, cut fine diagonal slits into the top of the leg of lamb. These slits must not be any deeper than 1 cm, and you should leave about 2 cm between each slit. Combine the oil, lemon juice and dried rosemary and brush it over the lamb. Leave to sit for 30 minutes and then dust the lamb with the sumac, to taste.

2 Cook the leg of lamb on a rack in a roasting pan in the oven for 10 minutes, then decrease the temperature to 180°C and cook until done to your liking. For rare, cook for approximately 60–70 minutes; for medium, cook for 70–90 minutes; for well done, cook for 100–110 minutes. Baste the lamb at least once during cooking. When done, remove from the oven and lift the lamb out to sit in a warm place for 15 minutes.

3 Drain any excess fat from the pan juices and put the roasting pan over medium heat on the stove top. Add the onion and cook for 1 minute. Stir in the garlic and tomato and pour in the wine; simmer for a few minutes. Mix the cornflour and stock together and pour into the pan, away from the heat. Return to the heat and stir briskly to incorporate the flour mixture. Stir until thickened. Season with salt and fresh rosemary, tip in any juices from the leg of lamb and stir in.

4 Carve the lamb and serve with lashings of the sauce and cooked seasonal vegetables of your choice.

TIP

When cooking with vegetables and you want to make good gravy, use some of the vegetable peelings to sit under the meat—say, onion and carrot peelings. This stops the meat from sitting in the fat (and from getting a burnt bottom). When the cooking is finished, remove cooked food, drain as much fat as you can away and then add wine or water and put the roasting pan back over heat. This will give you an instant stock to be thickened.

SERVES 4–6

2 kg leg of lamb, bone in

1 tablespoon olive oil

juice of $1/2$ lemon

1 tablespoon dried rosemary, crushed

30–60 g sumac spice

for the sauce

1 tablespoon finely chopped onion

5 cloves garlic, roughly chopped

1 small tomato, finely diced

1 cup (250 ml) red wine

1 tablespoon cornflour

$1/2$ cup (125 ml) beef or lamb stock (see Basics page 131) at room temperature

1 tablespoon chopped fresh rosemary

pot-roasted seasoned lamb shoulder

SERVES 4

1 shoulder of lamb, boned

1 cup fresh ciabatta (or other crusty bread) crumbs

1 tablespoon finely diced onion, pan-fried in butter to translucency stage

2 tablespoons roughly chopped macadamia nuts

$1/2$ teaspoon smoky paprika

1 tablespoon chopped fresh rosemary

1 egg, beaten

$1/2$ teaspoon salt

2 tablespoons butter

2 medium-sized onions, roughly diced

2 medium-sized carrots, roughly diced

$1/4$ cup (60 ml) chicken or lamb stock (see Basics pages 130 and 131)

Ciabatta bread is always so crusty, and in this recipe it somehow helps to give that special texture. I love macadamias with lamb, and the seasoning for this lamb dish is scrumptious, even on its own.

1 Trim the lamb of any excess fat and lay out flat, skin-side down, on a bench. If using string to tie up the shoulder, lay the meat on top of at least three long pieces of string.

2 Mix together the ciabatta crumbs, onion, macadamias, paprika, rosemary, egg and salt in a bowl. Work well with your hands. Pat the mixture onto the cut side of the lamb and then carefully roll the meat around the seasoning. Tie or skewer into place.

3 Put a cooking rack into the base of a suitable-sized lidded pan. Place the meat on the rack with butter dotted on top. Sprinkle the onions and carrots around the lamb, tip in the stock, cover and bring to the boil. Turn the heat right down and allow to cook slowly on the stove top. (It can be done in the oven, but pot-roasting demands constant basting, so it is easier on top of the stove.) Cook the lamb for 60–90 minutes, basting every 30 minutes until done. The internal temperature will be approximately 70°C when it is ready.

4 Lift the cooked meat from the pot. Ensure the vegetables are cooked; if not, continue to cook. Leave the meat to sit for 10 minutes, covered loosely with foil. Serve sliced with the cooked vegetables and a steamed green vegetable of your choice.

roasted chicken on onions with preserved lemons

PREHEAT OVEN TO 200°C

1 Wipe the chicken with kitchen towels and heat the oil in a deepish roasting pan on the stove top. Put the chicken in, breast down, and brown lightly. Remove from the pan and stuff the rind of one of the preserved lemons into the cavity of the chicken, along with the parsley. Truss to allow even cooking.

2 Add the onions to the pan and cook over medium heat for 3 minutes. When the onions are softened, pour in the chicken stock and bring to the boil. Remove from the heat and return the chicken to the pan. Put in the oven and cook for 20 minutes.

3 Cut the rind of the second lemon into small pieces. Remove the chicken from the oven, baste with the cooking liquid and scatter the lemon rind around the chicken. Return to the oven and continue cooking for 30 minutes, or until the chicken is done. Remove from the oven.

4 Lift the chicken onto a serving plate and return the pan to medium heat on the stove top. Add the peas and season with salt and freshly ground black pepper (remembering the preserved lemon can be salty). Cook for 3–4 minutes, or until the peas are done.

5 Slice the chicken into serving pieces, removing all meat from the carcass, and spoon the onions, peas and cooking liquid over. Serve with mashed sweet potatoes.

TIP

Use the leftover carcass as the base for an easy chicken stock (see Basics page 130).

SERVES 4

1.6 kg (no. 16) fresh free-range chicken

2 tablespoons olive oil

2 preserved lemons, rinds only and flesh discarded, well washed

4 sprigs fresh flat-leaf (Italian) parsley

3 large onions, cut into wedges

2 cups (500 ml) chicken stock (see Basics page 130)

1 cup fresh green peas

carpetbag *steak*

SERVES 4–6

1.5 kg piece fillet of beef, tail end

1 tablespoon butter

4 small mushrooms, stem removed,
  wiped and finely sliced

12 large natural oysters

1 tablespoon lemon juice

$1/2$ teaspoon finely grated or minced
  lemon zest

1 teaspoon green peppercorns

1 tablespoon brandy

$1/4$ teaspoon garam masala

$1/2$–1 cup fresh breadcrumbs

1 tablespoon butter melted
  with 1 tablespoon olive oil

As far as I know, this is an Australian invention—well, we will claim it as ours. It falls into the retro-cooking area and I love it. You can create variations by using smoked oysters, if you like.

PREHEAT OVEN TO 190°C

1 Cut the trimmed fillet lengthwise to butterfly it.

2 Bring the butter to foaming point in a frying pan and add the mushroom slices. Cook for 1 minute, add the oysters and cook for a further minute. Pour in the lemon juice and add the zest, peppercorns, brandy and garam masala. Cook for 1 minute more and remove from the heat.

3 Sprinkle in enough of the breadcrumbs to take up the juices and leave you with a paste-like filling. Cool and spoon this oyster filling down the centre of the beef fillet. Wrap the meat around it and tie into place with string, or skewer closed with toothpicks.

4 Seal the meat in the heated butter and oil, then sit on a rack in a roasting pan and roast in the oven for 40 minutes.

5 Remove and allow to rest for 10 minutes before slicing into rounds to serve with roasted potatoes and freshly steamed greens of your choice.

shaved *rump steak* and layered vegetable terrine

The 'point' or end of rump is one of my favourite cuts of meat—generally small enough for four, and with no connective bits to hamper slicing. This terrine makes a great starter on its own with a drizzle of vinaigrette.

PREHEAT OVEN TO 200°C

1 Trim the leek and use only the white part. Cut the flesh lengthwise and peel the individual leaves from the stem. Blanch in salted boiling water and cook for 1 minute. Lift from the water and run under cold water. Allow to cool.

2 Line a 22 cm x 11 cm x 6 cm terrine mould or bread tin with greaseproof paper or plastic wrap, then line this with the blanched leek leaves. They will become the outside wrapping for the terrine, so let the leaves hang out over the sides so they can be wrapped over the top once all the ingredients have been layered into the mould or tin.

3 Start to layer in the capsicums, kumera, eggplant, carrots, onion, tomatoes, cucumber, bread and basil leaves, drizzling every third layer with a little olive oil. Check for colour and do not have the same tones together—carrot and tomato do not look good on top of each other, for example. The tapenade-spread bread is best placed with a layer of tomato on top, as the bread will absorb the juice from the tomatoes.

4 Fold the leek leaves over the top of the terrine, cover with a piece of greaseproof paper or plastic wrap and top with a heavy weight—I use a foil-covered house brick. Refrigerate and press for at least one day.

5 To cook the meat, first seal it in a pan of very hot oil. Cook for 1 minute, then turn the meat over and sprinkle the sealed top with a little salt and ground black pepper. When sealed, lift the meat onto a cooking rack in a suitable baking tray and cook to medium—approximately 30–40 minutes. Once done to your liking, leave to sit for 10 minutes before carving. Retain the juices in the baking tray, deglaze with stock or red wine and leave to simmer.

6 To serve, tip the terrine onto a carving board, remove all paper or plastic wrap and slice into 3 cm thick pieces. Lie the pieces flat in the centre of each plate. Slice the meat very finely, gather it into bundles and place them beside the terrine. Spoon the pan juices over the meat and a little onto the terrine. Serve with a dressed green salad.

SERVES 4

for the terrine

1 large, fat leek

1 each of red, green and yellow capsicums, cheeks removed, char-grilled and skinned

1 long, straight kumera (orange sweet potato), peeled and cut into 5 mm thick strips and char-grilled

1 medium-sized eggplant, cut into 5 mm thick slices, sprayed with oil and char-grilled

2 medium-sized carrots, peeled and sliced into 5 mm thick strips and blanched

1 red onion, finely sliced

4–6 Roma tomatoes, flesh sliced from the core, cut into long strips

1–2 small Lebanese cucumbers, finely sliced lengthways

4–6 slices of good bread with crusts removed and spread with green olive tapenade

20 basil leaves

olive oil

1 kg point of rump, at room temperature

1 tablespoon vegetable oil

beef stock (see Basics page 131) or red wine, for deglazing

roasted *rib of beef* with sautéed potatoes and stewed mushrooms

Having a good relationship with your butcher is always useful, especially when you need special cuts of meat. Take this glorious dish for example. Ideally you need a standing rib roast with four ribs. Whether or not your butcher will be able to oblige will really depend on the size of the beast he has available at the time. If the beast is too large and a piece with four ribs is not available, just cook the meat as instructed anyway. Then, instead of carving the meat down each rib, you should simply cut the cooked meat from the bone in one piece and then slice it. Whichever way you have it, it is truly worthwhile, as this is a magnificent dish.

PREHEAT OVEN TO 220°C (FOR RARE AND MEDIUM) OR 200°C (FOR WELL DONE)

1 Tie the trimmed rib of beef with string to ensure even cooking. Tip the onion skins and celery and carrot trimmings into a suitable-sized roasting pan. Sit the beef on top, smear with butter, sprinkle with salt and ground black pepper and cook in oven for 10 minutes. Decrease the temperature to 200°C for rare and medium and 180°C for well done. For rare, cook for a further 30–40 minutes; for medium, cook for a further 50–70 minutes; for well done, cook for a further 110–130 minutes. Remove from the oven, lift out the meat and rest it, covered loosely with foil, for at least 15 minutes before slicing. Reserve the roasting pan contents.

2 Cook the mushrooms by melting the butter in a frying pan then adding the green onions and garlic. Cook for 1 minute and add the mushrooms, the demi glace and the red wine. Bring to the boil, then reduce to a simmer and cook for at least 1 hour. Add the marjoram and salt and cook for 10 minutes.

3 While the meat is resting, cook the potatoes. Heat the oil and butter in a frying pan and, when foaming, add the potatoes and toss to cook until browned. Move the slices around gently and let them crisp.

for the beef

Approx. 2 kg rib of beef, preferably with
  4 rib bones

onion skins, celery and carrot trimmings,
  or whole ones if trimmings not available

1 tablespoon butter

$^1/_2$ teaspoon salt

for the mushrooms

$1^1/_2$ tablespoons butter

60 g green onions, chopped

3 cloves garlic, minced

400 g assorted mushrooms, roughly chopped
  (use wild or exotic mushrooms like shiitake
  and porcini as well as regular ones)

300 ml demi glace (available from good butchers)

$^1/_4$ cup (60 ml) red wine

1 tablespoon chopped fresh marjoram

$^1/_2$ teaspoon salt

for the potatoes

2 tablespoons olive oil

1 tablespoon butter

400 g potatoes, peeled, cut into thick rounds
  and blanched

$^3/_4$ cup (185 ml) red wine

1 cup (250 ml) beef stock (see Basics page 131)

2 tablespoons butter, extra

4 Put the roasting tin and its contents back over medium heat on the stove top. When sizzling, add the red wine and beef stock and stir to incorporate the cooking sediment. Strain into a small saucepan and leave to simmer.

5 To serve, remove the string from the meat and cut down the bone. Divide the potatoes and mushrooms evenly among the individual plates and top with a slice of beef. Remove the pan juices from the heat and swirl in the butter (do not beat or whisk). When incorporated, spoon over the beef. Serve with selected mustards and cooked green vegetables of your choice.

roasted *rack of pork* with fennel and white turnips

SERVES 4

1.5 kg rack of pork, or rack of
  8 cutlets, rind removed

1 tablespoon vegetable oil

1 cup (250 ml) white wine mixed
  with 1 cup (250 ml) water

2 small fennel bulbs or 1 large one,
  halved and then sliced thinly

4 small white turnips, peeled and
  quartered

1 small onion, sliced

1 tablespoon salted butter

fresh dill, to taste, torn into small
  pieces

PREHEAT OVEN TO 200°C

1 Trim the pork and sprinkle with salt to taste. If the pork is large, you may have to cut the rack into two for easier handling. Your butcher will do this. Seal the meat in very hot oil in a frying pan and then leave to rest.

2 Pour the wine and water into a roasting pan and add the fennel, turnips and onion. Place this pan onto the bottom rack of the oven. Put the pork onto the rack above the turnips and fennel. Cook for 10 minutes, then reduce the oven temperature to 180°C and cook for 75 minutes or until done.

3 Test the pork to ensure it is cooked—the juices should run clear when a skewer is inserted and the internal temperature should read 75°C. When cooked, remove and keep in a warm place to rest. Meanwhile, add to the turnip mixture the butter, half the dill and salt and pepper to taste. Turn the vegetables over and cook for 10 minutes, then remove from the oven.

4 Serve the rack whole and slice at the table, or serve individually by spooning the turnips and fennel mixture into the centre of plates, slicing the pork into eight cutlets and serving two onto each plate, leaning against the vegetables. Spoon the juices from the turnips over the pork and sprinkle with the remaining dill. You may like to add other vegetables to give more colour and flavour. I serve mine with green peas.

veal *and fragrant vegetable pie*

I once featured this recipe in a winter column for the *Friday Magazine* that goes all round Australia. It received a marvellous reception and has gone on to be a dish that I do regularly at home. The pastry is fantastic.

PREHEAT OVEN TO 220°C

1 In a heavy-based saucepan, melt 1 tablespoon of the butter over medium heat. When the butter is foaming, add the onion and stir to cook for 2 minutes. Lift out of the pan and put in the other tablespoon of butter. Bring up to high heat and add the meat; this will need to be done in two batches. Stir to allow even browning of the meat.

2 Combine the cooked onion and meat in the saucepan and sprinkle in the flour. Stir the flour to coat the meat and pour in the stock and sherry. Add the turnip and parsnip and bring to the boil. Reduce to a simmer and cook for 1 hour, stirring occasionally to ensure the mixture is not sticking. When the meat is done, remove from the heat, stir in the tarragon and allow to cool for 3 hours before making the pie.

3 Prepare the pastry and leave to rest for 5 minutes before dividing into two. Roll out the first piece so it will line a greased pie dish. Invert an eggcup in the centre of the pastry base and spoon in the veal filling, then roll out the pastry lid. Brush the edge of the bottom piece of pastry with some of the beaten egg and top with the lid. Press the two edges together and then trim with the back of a knife. Crimp the edges with your thumb and fingers, or use a fork, dipping the tines in flour to prevent them sticking to the pastry.

4 Cut four holes in the pastry top, brush evenly with the egg and bake in the oven for 20 minutes, then lower the temperature to 180ºC to complete the cooking, which will take a further 30 minutes or until the pastry is golden brown. Serve with steaming hot vegetables.

TIP

When baking pastry, start on high so as to set the dough. Slow heat to start 'melts' the pastry, causing it to fall into the filling.

SERVES **4–6**

2 tablespoons butter

1 large onion, roughly chopped

1 kg stewing veal, diced into even
pieces

2 tablespoons plain flour

3 cups (750 ml) beef stock (see
Basics page 131) mixed with 1 cup
(250 ml) cooking sherry

1 small turnip, peeled and roughly
diced

2 medium-sized parsnips, peeled
and roughly diced

2 tablespoons chopped fresh
tarragon

1 quantity hot water pastry
(see Basics page 137)

1 egg, beaten

veal and pork *stuffed capsicums*

SERVES 4

4 large red capsicums, tops removed
and seeds scooped out; dice any
flesh that may be left over

250 g veal mince

250 g pork mince

1 cup cooked long-grain rice

1 small onion, finely diced

1 cup diced celery

2 cups (500 ml) pasta tomato sauce

1 cup (250 ml) beef stock
(see Basics page 131)

PREHEAT OVEN TO 180°C (OPTIONAL)

1 Wash out the capsicums with water.

2 Mix the meats well with half the diced capsicum, plus the rice, onion
and salt and white pepper to taste. Stuff into the capsicums. Roll any
leftover meat into balls around 3 cm in diameter.

3 Put half the celery into the base of a saucepan or ovenproof container
that will allow the capsicums to sit snugly together. Sprinkle over the
remaining capsicum and celery dice, mix the tomato sauce with the
stock and pour around and over the capsicums. Any meatballs you
may have can be placed in the cooking liquid.

4 Bring to the boil on the stove top. Reduce to a simmer, cover and cook
until done—around 45 minutes. If you prefer to use the oven, put the
container in after you have brought the ingredients to the boil. Cook
for 45 minutes.

5 When done, serve with mashed potatoes and cooked green vegetables
of your choice.

veal and mushroom moussaka

SERVES 4–6

2 tablespoons olive oil

1 medium-sized onion, roughly
  chopped

1 small carrot, peeled and chopped

500 g veal mince

1 tablespoon plain flour

1 cup (250 ml) chicken or beef stock
  (see Basics pages 130 and 131)

6 mushrooms, stems removed

1 large eggplant, sliced thickly,
  leached with salt and drained

1 cup (250 ml) pasta tomato sauce

1–2 cups plain yoghurt

2 eggs

2 tablespoons plain flour

$1/2$ cup grated cheddar cheese
  mixed with $1/4$ cup grated
  Parmesan cheese

This dish is cooked all round the Mediterranean and is capable of so many adaptations. This one can be eaten at room temperature with a salad, served cooled or reheated in the microwave. It can also be frozen.

PREHEAT OVEN TO 180°c

1 Heat the oil in a frying pan to medium and cook the onion and carrot for 2 minutes. Add the mince and mash to stop it from forming lumps. Sprinkle on the flour, stir in and pour in the stock. Bring to a simmer and cook for 5 minutes. Remove from the heat and allow to cool.

2 In a separate frying pan, quickly pan-fry the mushrooms, remove and then quickly fry the eggplant slices.

3 Spoon half the meat mixture into a suitable ovenproof dish. Layer in the mushrooms, top with the eggplant and then add the rest of the meat. Now spoon the tomato sauce over the top of the mixture. Sprinkle with salt and ground black pepper to taste.

4 Mix the yoghurt, eggs and flour together and spoon evenly over the ingredients in the ovenproof dish. Sprinkle with the cheese (add more if you want) and bake for 40 minutes or until the top is golden brown.

5 Serve hot or at room temperature, with green vegetables of your choice.

baked *beef-stuffed* mushrooms

1 Remove the stems from the mushrooms (save to use in stocks or soups). Wipe the outsides of the mushrooms with a damp cloth— do not peel.

2 Mix the mince, egg, onion, garlic and porcini mushrooms well. Add enough breadcrumbs to take up the moisture. Season with salt and pepper to taste.

3 Stuff the meat mixture into the cup of the mushrooms and mound it up. Press the mixture in well and place the mushrooms in a roasting pan. Bake for around 40 minutes, or until cooked.

4 Remove the roasting pan from the oven and lift the mushrooms off. Put the pan with its cooking liquids over high heat on the stove top and, when very hot, pour in the reserved porcini water and red wine and cook, stirring all the time, to incorporate the sediment from the base of the pan.

5 Serve the mushrooms with cooked vegetables of your choice and with the reduced cooking juices poured over the mushrooms.

SERVES 4

8 x 8–10 cm diameter mushroom caps

500 g lean beef mince

1 egg

$\frac{1}{2}$ medium-sized onion, finely diced

2 cloves garlic, minced

$\frac{1}{4}$ cup rehydrated roughly chopped porcini mushrooms, soaking water retained

$\frac{1}{2}$–1 cup dried breadcrumbs

$\frac{1}{2}$ cup (125 ml) red wine

chicken, ham and potato pie with mustard fruits

1 quantity shortcrust pastry
  (see Basics page 136)
250 g waxy potatoes, finely diced
250 g piece ham
350 g cooked chicken, preferably
  thigh meat
200 g sour cream
4 eggs, 3 beaten and 1 whole
mustard fruits (see Basics
  page 134)

PREHEAT OVEN TO 200°C

1 Prepare the pastry and refrigerate for 2 hours.

2 Cook the potatoes in salted boiling water until done—they must not be overcooked, otherwise they will go mushy in the pie. When done, strain and run under cold water to stop the cooking, then allow to cool.

3 Trim the ham of any fat and cut into dice about the same size as the potatoes. Do the same with the chicken. Combine the meats and potatoes in a bowl and then fold in the cream and the beaten eggs. Season with salt if necessary (the ham has a salt content and the chicken may well too, depending on how it was cooked initially).

4 Cut two-thirds of the pastry from the pastry ball and roll out to line an oil-sprayed 24 cm springform tin. Bring the pastry up over the edges of the tin and spoon or pour in the filling. Trim the edges of the pastry so that there is a 3 cm border around the top of the filling. Combine the trimmed pastry with the remaining portion and roll it out to form the lid of the pie.

5 Take the remaining egg and beat it. Brush the edges of the pastry in the tin with some of this egg and put the pastry lid on top. Crimp the edges together with a fork and then brush the top with the remaining egg. Cut four to six holes into the top of the pie and cook in the oven for 30 minutes. Reduce the heat to 180°C and cook for a further 40–50 minutes. An inserted skewer will come out clean when the filling is cooked. Leave the pie to cool in the tin.

6 Serve sliced into wedges with mustard fruits and a freshly tossed green salad.

ham, caramelised onions and blue cheese pizza

MAKES 20 GOOD SLICES

2 tablespoons olive oil

500 g brown onions, sliced

1 teaspoon dried thyme leaves

2 x 26 cm pizza bases, purchased
  from supermarket or homemade
  (see Basics page 137)

1 cup (250 ml) ready-made pizza
  tomato sauce

1 cup diced ham

100 g blue-vein cheese

PREHEAT OVEN TO 220°C

1 Make the caramelised onions by heating the oil in a heavy-based frying pan and adding the onions and thyme. Cook over medium heat with the lid on the pan for 10 minutes. Check the progress and stir frequently. Keep on cooking the onions until they go dark brown. (If they look like sticking to the pan, add a little more oil. Oil also helps in the preserving the onions if you do not use them all at one time.) Once cooked, cool and store in an airtight container in the refrigerator.

2 If making your own pizza bases, roll or press them out now and put them onto 2 x 26 cm pizza trays and leave to rest for 5 minutes. If using purchased pizza bases, have them at the ready.

3 Spread the tomato sauce onto the pizza bases to within 3 cm of the edge. Add as much of the caramelised onion as you like. Sprinkle over the ham and dot with blue cheese. Cook for 15 minutes in the oven.

4 Remove the pizzas from the oven and cut into wedges. Serve when cool enough to handle.

TIP

A secret to getting a crisp pizza base is to cook the pizzas on two paving bricks placed on the racks in the oven. They get really hot and will always crisp the pastry base.

basics

Every cookbook has one of these sections—it is for we poor authors who can't quite decide where to put certain recipes. For me, also, these recipes are useful for so many other dishes and for times when you're looking for a little inspiration for that certain accompaniment.

stocks

The beauty of leftover bones is that you can turn them into a delicious stock that can be kept in the freezer for weeks. Of course, if you don't have time to make your own stock you can purchase good stock these days in 'long-life' cartons from your supermarket. But there's nothing like the real thing. Here are three basic stocks for you.

chicken stock

MAKES APPROXIMATELY **8** CUPS (**2** L)
PREHEAT OVEN TO **200°C**

1 chicken carcass
1 large onion, chopped
1 tablespoon vegetable oil
1 stick celery, chopped
1 carrot, chopped
1 cup (250 ml) white wine (optional)
6 fresh parsley stems (optional)
3–4 cloves (optional)
1 bay leaf

1 Place the chicken carcass in a roasting pan and brown quickly in the oven—about 20–30 minutes.

2 Meanwhile, brown the onion in the oil in a stockpot over low heat on the stove top. Add the carcass, celery and carrot, cover with approximately 12–16 cups (3–4 L) of water and bring to a simmer. Cook for 1 hour. If you wish you can add other flavourings to the pot, including white wine, parsley stems, cloves and bay leaf. Do so when you add the water.

3 Simmer the stock for 2 hours, scooping off any foam that appears at the top.

4 Strain and pour into a storage container. If freezing, use 2 cup (500 ml) containers so you know how much you have on hand.

NOTE *This stock is honey-coloured and good for brown soups or sauces. If you want to use the stock for white dishes, say a cream of cauliflower soup, you'll need a white chicken stock. This is achieved by not browning the bones to start with, and simmering for only 1 hour.*

lamb stock

MAKES APPROXIMATELY **8 CUPS (2 L)**
PREHEAT OVEN TO **200°c**

1 kg any uncooked lamb bones with the raw meat that may be left on them

2 onions, cut in halves with skins on

2 carrots, roughly chopped

2 sticks celery, roughly chopped

1 cup (250 ml) red or white wine

6 fresh parsley stems

1 Place the bones and onions in a roasting pan and cook in the oven until the onions are browned—about 45 minutes.

2 Lift the bones and onions into a stockpot, cover with approximately 12–16 cups (3–4 L) of water and bring to the boil. Add the carrots and celery.

3 Meanwhile, heat the roasting pan on the stove top until very hot and smoking. Deglaze the pan by pouring in the wine. Stir for 2 minutes to incorporate the cooking sediment and then pour into the stockpot.

4 Add parsley stems to the stockpot. Keep the stock simmering for at least 2 hours. Scoop any foam off the top that may appear during cooking.

5 Strain and keep in an airtight container in the fridge, or freeze in measured amounts. I usually use 2 cup (500 ml) containers.

beef stock

You can substitute veal bones for the beef bones to make a fine veal stock.

MAKES APPROXIMATELY **8 CUPS (2 L)**
PREHEAT OVEN TO **220°c**

2 kg beef bones, sawn into small pieces (ask the butcher)

2 onions, sliced into three rounds each (leave skins on)

2 carrots, roughly chopped

1 stick celery, roughly chopped

1 cup (250 ml) red wine

1 tablespoon black peppercorns

6 fresh parsley sprigs and their stems

1 bay leaf

1 Place the bones in a roasting pan and add the onions. Brown in the oven for 30–45 minutes, or until deep brown in colour but not burnt.

2 Lift the bones and onions into a stockpot and add the carrots and celery. Cover with approximately 12–16 cups (3–4 L) of water. Deglaze the pan with the wine and pour onto the bones.

3 Add the whole peppercorns, parsley sprigs and their stems and the bay leaf. Bring to the boil and then simmer for at least 2 hours.

4 Strain and use when needed. Store in 2 cup (500 ml) containers if freezing.

cumberland sauce

This wonderful old English sauce was used extensively when I first started cooking. It is making a return, as it is simple to prepare and a perfect accompaniment to grilled and cold meats.

MAKES APPROXIMATELY **1 CUP (250ML)**

4 tablespoons redcurrant jelly

2 teaspoons smooth Dijon mustard

zest of 1 orange, blanched

$1/2$ teaspoon dried ground ginger

$1/4$ teaspoon cayenne pepper

$1/2$ cup (125 ml) port wine

1 Heat all the ingredients, except for the port wine, in a saucepan over very low heat until all have melted.

2 Stir in the wine and combine.

3 Serve at room temperature.

tomato relish

Tomatoes continually amaze me with their adaptability, suiting everything from simple salads to jams and, as this recipe shows, a quick relish. This will keep for at least two weeks in the refrigerator and is best kept for two days before first using.

MAKES **3–4 CUPS (750 ML–1 L)**

6 large semi-ripe tomatoes, roughly diced

1 large onion, finely chopped

3 cloves garlic, finely chopped

2 tablespoons white sugar

$1/2$ cup (125 ml) white vinegar

1 tablespoon mustard powder

1 tablespoon curry powder (see page 138)

1 bay leaf

6 cloves

1 cinnamon stick

1 teaspoon salt

1 Put all the ingredients, except the salt, into a suitable-sized saucepan and simmer until the onion is cooked and the flavours are combined. Stir constantly, especially when the liquid is nearly evaporated. (It is at this time that the relish can stick and burn on the bottom of the pan.)

2 Remove from the heat, stir in the salt and cool before storing in sterilised airtight containers.

zucchini bread

I first used this recipe on Mike Carlton's show on 2GB in the early 1980s. It was immensely popular, and when I used it again on the 'Today' show much later, I had thousands of requests for the recipe.

MAKES 2 LOAVES
PREHEAT OVEN TO 170°C

375 g small zucchinis, grated
3 eggs, beaten
1 tablespoon white sugar
1 teaspoon vanilla essence
$1/2$ teaspoon salt
3 cups self-raising flour, sifted
1 teaspoon powdered nutmeg
1 cup walnuts, crumbled
olive oil spray

1 Place the zucchini, eggs, sugar, vanilla essence and salt in a bowl. Stir to combine well.

2 Fold in the flour, nutmeg and walnuts and leave to sit for 5 minutes.

3 Spray two bread tins (each 21 cm x 11 cm x 6 cm) with olive oil. Spoon the zucchini mixture into the tins and bake in the oven for 1 hour, or until a skewer comes out clean.

4 Leave the loaves in their tins for 15 minutes to cool, then turn onto a cooling rack to cool before slicing.

apple and ginger sauce

MAKES 4 CUPS (1 L)

4 green apples, peeled, cored and roughly chopped
1 tablespoon grated fresh ginger,
2 teaspoons dried ground ginger
2 tablespoons raw sugar
6 cloves
1 star anise

1 Put all ingredients into a suitable-sized saucepan and bring to the boil. Reduce to a simmer to allow the apples to break down to a sauce—about 5–10 minutes.

2 Remove the star anise and cloves and mash the remaining mixture to a runny sauce.

poached garlic aioli

I like to poach the garlic to lose that strong, sometimes pungent flavour that has an unattractive bite to it. You can do this recipe in the food processor or by hand.

MAKES $3/4$–1 CUP (185–250 ML)

6 large cloves garlic, poached in boiling water for 2 minutes

1/2 teaspoon salt

2 egg yolks

1/2 cup (125 ml) olive oil

1 teaspoon lemon juice

1 Put the garlic, salt and egg yolks in a food processor and work for 30 seconds. When light gold in colour, start to drip the oil down the feeder shoot. As it takes, you can add the oil at a fine drizzle until finished.

2 To store, put into a sterilised airtight container and keep for no longer than five days. Stir in the lemon juice as you serve.

---

garlic confit

6 heads garlic

6 sprigs fresh thyme

vegetable oil

1 Cut a third off the garlic heads, from the sprouting end, and discard. Pack the garlic into a saucepan, root down, along with the sprigs of thyme, and cover with the oil.

2 Cook over very low heat on the stove top for 1 hour. (The slower the cooking, the more flavour is released.) The garlic will brown slightly.

3 Remove from the heat, cool and then pack the garlic into a suitable storage container with the oil. The garlic is great crushed and on heated ciabatta, or in mayonnaise. The oil is sensational for salad dressings and cooking.

---

mustard fruits

I love this accompaniment. The amount of vinegar you use depends on how dry the fruit is and also how much acidity you like.

100 g glacé fruits, roughly chopped

15 g mustard seeds

60–100 ml white vinegar

1 cinnamon stick

nutmeg, grated

1 Combine all the ingredients in an airtight container and put the lid on.

2 Shake the fruits well and invert several times. Leave to sit in a cool, dark spot for at least a week before use, turning the container regularly in this time and adding more vinegar if needed. These mustard fruits will keep for at least six weeks.

potato gnocchi

I have watched great cooks and chefs make this wonderful Italian speciality for years. Stefano Manfredi's mother, Franka, is an absolute whiz at it, as is famous Noosa chef Garry Flynn. Once you have mastered this recipe you will love it as much as I do.

1 kg medium-sized Desiree potatoes
1 teaspoon salt
300–325 g plain flour, sifted

1 Cover the potatoes (skins on) with cold water and bring to the boil. Reduce to a simmer and cook until done—around 15–20 minutes. The potatoes are cooked with their skins on so they don't absorb the cooking water.

2 Drain and leave to cool enough to handle, then remove the skin from the potatoes. Mash finely and tip onto a floured bench.

3 Sprinkle on the salt and then start to incorporate the flour a little at a time. Use the heel of your hand to work the flour into the potato. Use as much flour as is needed to take up the liquid in the potatoes.

4 Cut the dough into eight small pieces and then roll out to sausage shapes to your desired thickness. Cut into bite-sized pieces and press with a fork to give ridges that will capture the sauce as you eat.

5 Bring a large saucepan of water to the boil. Reduce to a simmer, shake excess flour off the gnocchi and cook in the simmering water until the gnocchi float to the top. You will have to do this in three batches. Lift out with a slotted spoon and run under cold water if not using immediately.

6 Store on oiled trays if made the day before. Reheat in boiling water (or in the microwave) and serve with grated Parmesan cheese, good extra-virgin olive oil and roughly chopped or torn basil leaves. Gnocchi can also be served with a good veal and tomato stew.

mint pesto

This is a remarkably refreshing paste. Use it straight away, as the mixture goes dark very quickly. If you like it to be more liquid than it is, simply add more oil.

MAKES 1 CUP (250 ML)

1 cup fresh mint sprigs, washed and tightly packed
1 tablespoon roasted pine nuts
$1/3$ cup (80 ml) walnut oil
1 large clove garlic, crushed
40 g Parmesan cheese, finely grated

1 Place the mint and nuts in a food processor and blend for 30 seconds. Pour the oil in slowly down the feeder shoot, then add the garlic and cheese to make a rough paste.

2 Use immediately or store under a film of olive or walnut oil.

spinach, rocket and cashew nut pesto

MAKES 2 CUPS (500 ML)

100 g raw cashews
1 cup spinach leaves, trimmed and washed
1 cup rocket leaves, trimmed and washed
1 cup (250 ml) olive oil
$1/2$ cup Parmesan cheese, finely grated
$1/2$ teaspoon salt

1 Lightly brown the cashews in a frying pan. Leave to cool.

2 Pack the spinach, rocket and cashews into a food processor and finely chop. Keep the motor going and gradually add the oil, Parmesan and salt.

3 Spoon out the pesto into a storage container. Check for seasoning and add black pepper to taste. (Note that the rocket, especially if it is not hydroponically grown, can be quite spicy and so you may not need pepper.)

shortcrust pastry

$1^{1}/2$ cups plain flour, sifted
100 g butter, very cold and chopped
1 egg, beaten
2–3 tablespoons cold water

1 Make the pastry by rubbing the flour and butter to breadcrumb stage. Do this with your fingertips or in a food processor.

2 Tip in the egg and a little of the water and work the pastry into a firm dough. I generally use a blunt knife to do this. You may have to add all the water, depending on how the dough is holding together.

3 Knead the dough quickly and lightly. Form into a ball, cover with plastic wrap and refrigerate for 2 hours.

hot water pastry

This pastry used to be made with lard and would produce a wonderful
sheen. I use butter in this recipe, but use lard if you prefer.

125 g butter, melted

400 g plain flour

1 Place the melted butter in a saucepan with 200 ml of hot water.
Bring to a simmer.

2 Tip in the flour and remove from the heat. Stir in with a wooden spoon
and then turn out onto a floured bench.

3 Knead the pastry for about 3 minutes, or until it is smooth. Allow the
pastry dough to rest for at least 5 minutes before using.

basic pizza dough

MAKES 1 X 26–30 CM THICK PIZZA BASE OR 2 X 26 CM THIN BASES

$1\frac{1}{2}$ teaspoons active dried yeast

$\frac{1}{2}$ teaspoon white sugar

3 cups plain flour

1 teaspoon salt

1 tablespoon olive oil

1 Mix the yeast and sugar with 1 cup (250 ml) of lukewarm water in a large
glass bowl and leave to sit in a warm place until it starts frothing—
around 10 minutes.

2 Sift the flour and salt onto the yeast, pour in the oil and combine.
This can be done with a dough hook on an electric mixer, by hand
or with a wooden spoon.

3 Once combined, knead well for at least 5 minutes. Place in a lightly
greased bowl, cover with a tea towel and leave in a warm place to
double in size—around 90–120 minutes.

4 The dough then needs to be 'knocked back', which is done by literally
punching it with your fist to release all the air trapped in the dough.
Tip the dough out onto a lightly floured bench and knead again, then
roll out to fit the pizza tray you want.

curry powder

MAKES APPROX. 2 CUPS

250 g dried chillies

125 g coriander seeds

60 g cumin seeds

1 cardamom pod, split and seeds removed

1 teaspoon fenugreek seeds

1 x 5 cm cinnamon stick

1 Over low heat, dry-fry all the spices, except for the cinnamon, until dark brown. Do not burn. Remove from the heat and break the cinnamon stick into the mixture.

2 When cool enough, either pound all the ingredients in a mortar and pestle or in a spice grinder.

3 Store in an airtight jar.

peanut green curry paste

MAKES 1 CUP

1 teaspoon cumin seeds

2 teaspoons coriander seeds

2 green onions, finely sliced

3 cloves garlic, roughly chopped

1x3 cm piece fresh ginger, peeled and roughly chopped

1 teaspoon salt

1 x 20 cm long piece of lemongrass, white part only

6 small red chillies, seeded and roughly chopped

3 kaffir lime leaves, vein removed and finely chopped

1 teaspoon roasted shrimp paste

2 tablespoons raw peanuts, roughly chopped

1 Dry-fry the cumin and coriander seeds over medium heat for 1 minute or until lightly browned. Cool and then grind into a powder using a mortar and pestle or a spice grinder.

2 Combine the green onions, garlic, ginger, salt, lemongrass, chillies, kaffir lime leaves, shrimp paste and peanuts in a food processor and work until a rough paste. Alternatively, pound these ingredients using a mortar and pestle. When a paste is forming, add the cumin and coriander powder and work into a finer paste.

3 Store in an airtight container in the fridge and use within three or four days.

jellied beetroot and coriander terrine

Jellies are back in fashion again. In my youth, this dish was served everywhere, and in the early nineties I used this dish as the base of a main course of lamb in the United States.

juice of 1 lime

1 tablespoon port wine

6 cloves

2 tablespoons finely chopped fresh coriander leaves

1 tablespoon finely chopped fresh flat-leaf (Italian) parsley leaves

$1/2$ teaspoon salt

$1/8$ teaspoon cayenne pepper

$1^1/2$ tablespoons gelatine

$1/2$ cup (125 ml) cold water

500 g cooked beetroot, grated

1 Combine the lime juice, wine and $3^1/2$ cups (875 ml) of water in a saucepan. Bring to the boil with the cloves, coriander, parsley, salt and cayenne pepper, then reduce to a simmer.

2 Meanwhile, soften the gelatine in the cold water and melt in a pan over the simmering liquids. When the gelatine is melted, remove both pans from the heat and cool for 1 minute. Stir the melted gelatine into the spicy liquid, cover and allow to cool for 10 minutes.

3 Put the beetroot into a suitable container (a glass bowl or mould) and then strain the cooled liquid over it. With a fork or similar (I use a chopstick), move the beetroot around so the gelatine is well combined.

4 Refrigerate overnight and serve as required.

how best to cook each meat cut

Here is an at-a-glance table to tell you what the best ways are to cook each cut of meat.

	STIR-FRIES AND SAUTÉS	BARBECUES AND GRILLS	BRAISES AND CASSEROLES	ROASTS AND BAKED DISHES
LAMB	Loin, boneless	Chump chops	Corned leg	Leg, bone in
	Chump chops	Cutlets	Chump chops	Leg, boned and tied
	Leg chops	Leg chops	Leg chops	Crown roast
	Tenderloin (fillets)	Loin chops	Shoulder	Shoulder, bone in or boned and seasoned
	Cutlets	Boneless loin	Best neck chops	Rack
		Sausages	Shanks	Saddle
		Racks	Chump chops	Loin, boned
		Mince		
BEEF	Rump steak	Rump steak	Chuck steak	Point of rump
	Scotch fillet	Scotch fillet	Round steak	Striploin (sirloin)
	Striploin (sirloin)	Tenderloin	Brisket	Tenderloin
	Oyster blade	T-bone	Corned meats	Whole blade (slow-roasted)
	Eye round	Striploin (sirloin)	Shin meat	Rib roast
	Sausages	Sausages	Sausages	
	Tenderloin	Hamburger mince	Chuck tender	
	Mince			
VEAL	Schnitzel steaks	Chops	Legs	Leg
	Cutlets	Tenderloin	Stuffed breasts	Tenderloin
	Tenderloin	Schnitzels	Rolled shoulders	Shoulders, boned and rolled
			Shin meat—osso buco	Rack
			Veal tongue	
POULTRY	Duck breast fillet	Duck breast fillet	Big ducks	Whole chicken
	Turkey breast	Turkey steaks	Turkey hindquarter	Boned and rolled chicken
	Chicken breast fillet	Chicken breast fillet	Bigger, older chickens	Chicken Maryland
	Chicken thigh fillet	Chicken Maryland	Chicken thigh cutlets	Whole duck
	Chicken thigh cutlet	Chicken thigh fillet	Chicken Maryland	Duck Maryland
			Chicken legs	Turkey buffe
				Whole turkey
PORK	Fillet	Tenderloin	Pumped leg	Leg
	Loin, boneless	Spare ribs (belly)	Diced forequarter	Loin, boneless
	Spare ribs (belly)	Spare ribs (babyback)	Whole chump	Shoulder, boned
	Sausages	Loin, boneless	Diced leg meat	Rack
	Medallions	Chops/cutlets	Sausages	
		Mince	Neck	

glossary

baste—To brush with cooking juices or a marinating medium.

blanch—To immerse an ingredient into boiling water to soften or break down the structure of the item. Generally the item is 'refreshed' by immersing it in cold or iced water to stop the cooking process.

butterfly or butterflied—The process of cutting a thickish item down the centre to open it out like butterfly wings. Generally makes the item flatter for more even cooking, or allows you to stuff it with a filling.

ciabatta—A flattish, crusty Italian bread with an open (bubbles) structure inside the bread.

cinnamon stick—The dried curled bark of the cinnamon tree, also known as cinnamon quills or curls. This spice comes in a powdered form as well.

confit—A term used to refer to all types of meats cooked in their own fat and then preserved/stored in the fat until ready for use. The fat prevents the air from coming in contact with the meat and thus putrefying it.

deglaze—A process whereby a liquid (e.g. stock, water, wine) is poured into a preheated cooking pan containing drained cooking sediment and stirred over high heat. The stirring lets the cooking sediment come into the solution and thus impart more flavour.

demi glace—A thickish brown sauce that is reduced with beef stock, mushroom trimmings and fortified wine (e.g. Madeira, dry sherry). Can be used as a base for many other sauces.

Desiree potato—A longish, oval-shaped potato with a pink skin and yellowy, waxy flesh. Suitable for baking or boiling.

dry-fry—To cook items without any cooking medium such as fat, oil or stock. The process intensifies the flavours being fried.

eschalot—A smaller, more compact onion from the onion family. Some think it is easier to digest.

garlic head—All the individual pieces, known as cloves, which form one whole head of garlic.

green onion—In Australia, we have confusion, as we often call it a spring onion or shallot. It is in fact a long, green and white thin stem with a mild onion flavour.

harissa—An extremely fiery and pungently hot paste from Tunisia. It is made from dried chillies, garlic, paprika and various other spices and herbs.

kecap manis—A sweet Indonesian soy sauce. Can be thick or thin.

leaching—A process whereby salt is sprinkled over a food (like eggplant slices) to extract the bitterness. Generally the salted slices are left to sit for 30 minutes, then washed to remove the brownish liquid. The slices are then patted dry and cooked.

mirin—A Japanese sweetened rice wine for cooking.

porcini mushrooms—Also known as cep or boletus mushrooms, these are normally dried and soaked before use. They are very popular in French and Italian cooking.

preserved lemons—Lemons which have been cut into sections, massaged with salt and then packed into a sterilised container with more salt. These are left for at least one month before use. Use the skin only.

ras el hanout—A blend of many spices that can remind you of a curry but can be spicy and fragrant. For more information, refer to Ian Hemphill's book *Spice Notes*.

refresh—To run a blanched item under cold water.

rest—To leave a cooked item (usually a roast cut of meat) to sit in a warm place, covered loosely with foil, so the juices set. A minimum of 10 minutes is required.

rissoni pasta— Rice-shaped pasta, sometimes called 'orzo'.

rub—To massage spices into an item, or the spices themselves.

seal—To put meat on a very hot heat source to trap the juices in by forming a crust.

season—To add spices or salt to the cooking item. The term can also mean a filling to go inside a chicken, or to be wrapped inside a flat piece of meat.

shiitake mushrooms—Famous Japanese mushrooms with bright brown tops and whitish underbellies. They have a delicious and slightly pungent flavour, and a firm texture.

silver (on meat)—Also known as silver skin, this is a tissue that coats a meat muscle. It must be removed to prevent 'curling' of the meat during cooking.

sirloin plate—Boneless sirloin.

sumac—The ground berry or the leaves of the sumac tree. Also seen as sumach or sumak. The spice is pinkish to burgundy in colour, and tastes fruity and salty.

tahini—A paste made from white sesame seeds. It is used in many Mediterranean dishes.

tamarind pulp—The seedpod to the tree of the same name (*Tamarindus indica*), which usually comes as a pulp with the seeds in. This needs to be soaked in water to turn into a paste and then strained to remove the seeds. There is also a liquid paste which is easier to use. Tamarind is used in Asian cooking to provide a sour taste which will balance out other flavours.

truss—To tie a chicken with string so that it is compact. When the legs and wings are tied close to the body, this allows for even cooking.

index

Thomas C. Lothian Pty Ltd
132 Albert Road, South Melbourne 3205
www.lothian.com.au

National Library of Australia Cataloguing-in-Publication data:

Howard, Peter, 1947–
Meat!

ISBN 0 7344 0381 X.

Cookery (Meat). I. Filshie, Joe. II. Title.

641.66

Cover and text design: Peta Nugent
Photography: Joe Filshie
Styling: Georgie Dolling
Home Economist: Justine Poole

Colour reproduction by Digital Imaging Group, Port Melbourne
Printed in Singapore by SNP SPrint Pte Ltd

Thanks to the following for supplying props:
Accoutrement, Bayswiss, Country Road, Lincraft, Live This, Maytag, Smeg, Witchery